THE
SACRED
PLATE

Recipes for
Abundant Living

Sarah Vie

This book is dedicated to you, the reader, to remind you that all things are possible.

Published by La Vie Press

Hardcover ISBN: 9798218429256

Cover and interior design by Liz Schreiter
Edited and produced by Reading List Editorial
ReadingListEditorial.com

CONTENTS

PART I
SCARCITY, ABUNDANCE, AND THE WAY WE EAT

FROM SCARCITY TO ABUNDANCE. 3

THE CONNECTION BETWEEN AN ABUNDANT MINDSET AND FOOD. 9

THE ENERGY THAT WE HOLD. 13

PART II
THE ENERGY CENTERS

THE ROOT CAUSE. 19

YOUR SEXY SACRAL . . . 39

YOUR GUTSY GUT. 61

HELLO, HEART 83

SPEAK YOUR MIND,
FIND YOUR TRUTH 103

FEAR IS IN THE EYE
OF THE BEHOLDER 123

CROWNING GLORY. . . .143

PART III
INTO SACRED ABUNDANCE

IT ALL ADDS UP 168

ACKNOWLEDGMENTS 172

PART I

SCARCITY, **ABUNDANCE**, AND THE WAY WE EAT

CHAPTER 1

FROM SCARCITY TO ABUNDANCE

*I*f you're reading this book, you likely have a strong interest in the concept of abundance. Maybe you're frustrated with your current situation. I can relate; I have spent a major part of my life feeling limited and unsure of how to break free. My journey was shaped by a scarcity mindset and the decisions I made as a result of it. I always knew deep down that there was more to life than what I was experiencing, but I lacked the knowledge and understanding of how to attract and manifest the abundance that was waiting for me.

Initially, my understanding of abundance was solely based on money. I believed that if I had enough money, I would be considered abundant. But I was mistaken. I had no knowledge of the power of vibration, frequency, and energy in attracting abundance into my life. I simply thought that if I appeared wealthy or earned a great deal of money, I would be abundant. But my perspective was completely off.

Shifting my mindset was crucial in determining the path I chose to take in life. You see, we can either travel down a road paved with scarcity and limitations, or we can opt for a path filled with abundance and expansion at every turn. The beauty is that, at any given moment, we have the power to change our direction. We can always choose to wake up feeling the weight of what life lacks or to awaken to the endless richness that life has to offer. This wealth is available to all of us if we shift our perspective and see the world through a lens of abundance.

I struggled to comprehend exactly what needed to change for me to experience life differently. The feelings of scarcity, unworthiness, and inadequacy had become so deeply ingrained within me that they felt as familiar as an old, worn-out sweater. Yet, as time passed, that identity no longer fit comfortably; it felt outdated and constricting.

At times, we can find ourselves oblivious to the existence of alternative paths in life. We become so enmeshed with a particular energy that we fail to recognize its origins and whether it truly aligns with our essence or not. Consider this: if a member of your family harbors feelings of scarcity within their being, that same energy can imprint itself onto your DNA, affecting your own energetic makeup. I've delved deep into research to learn about the intricate layers of generational trauma and discovered a profound revelation: we can carry the burdens of three generations' worth of unhealed energy within us. It's remarkable how interconnected our familial energies and our selves truly are.

My perception of abundance had been shaped by the experiences and beliefs passed down through generations in my family. Like layers woven into my DNA, I carried the echoes of my mother's upbringing in wartime England, during a time of rationing. Visiting her tiny cottage, I witnessed firsthand the remnants of scarcity—bits of butter carefully preserved, a testament to a time when extravagance was a luxury beyond reach. Beliefs about scarcity and deservingness were imprinted in my very being, shaping my relationship with abundance and worth.

When I was a child, despite the outward appearance of privilege, my family often faced a precarious financial reality, marked by late payments and bill collectors knocking on our doors. I can vividly recall my father's urgent plea for silence, directing my brother, sister, and me to stay quiet and hidden until the men in their polished suits had departed. It was our signal to wait until they were gone before we dared to address the looming stack of bills. I grappled with conflicting messages about what we could afford and what I believed I deserved, perpetuating a cycle of confusion and doubt. I internalized the belief that my desires for more were selfish, potentially taking away from others in my family. These childhood perceptions clouded my understanding of our true financial situation and left me questioning the validity of my own desires.

It's crucial to understand the pivotal role our thoughts play in shaping the energy we carry within our bodies. Our thoughts are like seeds that germinate within the fertile soil of our energy centers, influencing our emotional and physical well-being in profound ways. By acknowledging and addressing the roots of these inherited energies, we can embark on a transformative journey toward healing and liberation. Through self-awareness and intentional practices, we can untangle ourselves from the grip of ancestral wounds, reclaiming our autonomy and forging a path toward holistic wellness.

Amidst the shadows of doubt, there is hope. We have the power to release these energetic cords of our past, freeing ourselves from the grip of inherited beliefs and experiences. The journey begins with awareness—the recognition of the sensations and discomfort that arise when we confront specific memories or experiences.

To facilitate this release, I offer a powerful visualization technique: the Energy Cord and Seed Release method. Through deep introspection and focused breathing, we can identify the emotions and traumas connected to our past experiences. With a golden sword of intention and determination, we sever the cords that bind us to these outdated narratives, making space for new growth and abundance to flourish.

A Quick Release: Energy Cord and Seed Release Method

The Energy Cord and Seed Release method is a powerful visualization you can use when you feel as if you're blocked from receiving. You know what that sensation in your body feels like. Maybe you feel exhausted daily or unmotivated to try anything new or as if you are walking through a deep fog and you feel unclear about how to step through it. If you just feel off, you most likely are stuck.

> Sit comfortably with your eyes gently closed and take deep, healing breaths from your belly. Witness the rise and fall of your chest and stomach.
>
> In your mind's eye, think of an instance or scene from your childhood that still fills you with an emotion. Allow that emotion to settle in. Let it arise in your body. Get to know it. Allow it to be there. Be friends with it. This sensation is connected to a childhood trauma that you experienced in your past. Where does this sensation show up? Is it in your heart chakra or in your solar plexus?
>
> Wherever it shows up, bring your focus and your breath there. You no longer have to hold onto that anymore. Holding onto it is blocking what you want.
>
> Now that you have connected to what you desire to let go of, we are going to release this energy that you have attached to it. In your mind's eye, envision a golden sword. This sword can be as big as you want it to be. See the way it unfolds in your mind. This sword is very sharp and has magic powers to help you let go of whatever is blocking your magnetic source.
>
> Now, imagine a thick cord connected to that sensation you are feeling in that spot in your body. That cord presents the past—the trauma you have endured. That cord is no longer needed. It's almost rotted, it's so old. Even though it's rotten, it still has a charge connected to it. We are going to cut the cord together so you can make room for what you want to manifest. So, let's create that rich image of the cord connected to that place in your body.
>
> See your sharp, golden sword in your dominant hand. Feel it there. See it in front of you. Believe that you can release it now. Good.
>
> Now, I'm going to count backward, and on the count of five you will see yourself cutting that cord from your past with your magical golden sword.
>
> Take a deep breath in and out.
>
> Five.
>
> Four.

Three.

Two.

One.

Cut.

Feel the release. Feel the lightness now within your soul. Make sure you have cut all the way through.

If you feel as if you need to cut again, repeat the image until you feel lightness.

Take a deep breath again. In and out. When you're ready, you can open your eyes to the present moment, to your new inner energy. Ah!

INNER FEELINGS ATTRACT ABUNDANCE

Our society bombards us with images we perceive as symbols of abundance. We are captivated by the expensive designer clothing displayed in stores on Fifth Avenue, the luxurious cars that zoom through the streets of Malibu or Beverly Hills, the extravagant mansions with foyers larger than most houses, and the dazzling diamonds that sparkle in the sunlight. We are easily influenced by the lives portrayed by celebrities on reality TV, and we fall victim to what I like to call the "Kardashian disease." We compare our lives to the extravagant, materialistic lifestyles we see, and we can't help but feel inadequate. We strive to be like them, to attain their level of material wealth. I, too, was drawn into this mindset. As a young girl, I was misled by the misconception that abundance was solely about material possessions. I failed to grasp the true essence of abundance, which lies in the inner feeling it evokes. Abundance is not something tangible that can be measured by possessions alone. It is an inner state of being that attracts and manifests what we truly desire. It is the intangible beliefs we hold that ultimately shape the tangible things we attract into our lives.

Here's a list of what abundance is to me

Flowers in my hotel room or bedroom

Peace and calm in the morning

Drinking water

Sitting and enjoying a cup of coffee in the morning with no interruptions

Exercise and movement

Wearing perfume or essential oils before bed

Listening when someone is speaking

Eating slowly

Freedom of thought

Organizing a closet and purging what doesn't fit anymore

Looking into someone's eyes and seeing their soul

Prayers of gratitude before beginning to eat

Sitting down with some hot tea in the afternoon and a small, sweet treat and reflecting on my day

Taking a moment to listen to children's laughter

Listening to birds singing in the morning

Making my bed hospital style before my day begins

Cleaning my house while listening to music or an uplifting podcast

Listening to soft music as I wake up in the morning

Getting into bed after washing the sheets

Opening my window at night and smelling fresh air

Spending more and more time being silent and in solitude

Making my house smell delicious

Enjoying a bath bomb or bubble bath

Taking a long shower with lots of lather

Dressing neatly and comfortably on a plane

Being kind and helpful

Acknowledging the elderly and making them feel seen

Watching a sunrise or sunset and meeting myself in the glow

Loving someone with all my heart without hesitation

Smiling at strangers to brighten their day

Looking at my reflection in the mirror without any judgment

Giving myself a high five in the morning

Saying good morning to a stranger

Paying it forward

Giving someone a generous tip

Nutritious, abundant, colorful food

Do you feel the abundant energy in this list?

THE IMPORTANCE OF ABUNDANCE

Feeling the energy of abundance is of paramount importance in our lives, as it shapes our mindset, influences our experiences, and ultimately determines the quality of our existence. When we embrace abundance, we cultivate a positive and expansive mindset that opens us up to endless possibilities. Rather than dwelling on scarcity and lack, an abundant mindset allows us to focus on the abundance that already exists in our lives, whether it be in the form of opportunities, resources, nourishment, relationships, or personal strengths.

The importance of abundance lies in its transformative power. When we shift our perspective from scarcity to abundance, we tap into a limitless source of creativity, resilience, and gratitude. We begin to see the world through a different lens, one that is filled with optimism and possibilities. This shift in mindset not only enhances our overall well-being but also empowers us to act toward our goals and dreams. Moreover, embracing the energy of abundance enables us to attract more abundance into our lives. The law of attraction states that like attracts like, and by aligning ourselves with abundance, we magnetize opportunities, resources, and positive experiences. When we believe in our inherent worth and abundance, we radiate confidence and attract circumstances and people that align with our desires and aspirations.

Abundance is not limited to material possessions. It extends to all aspects of our lives, including our health, personal growth, and happiness. We appreciate the richness of life's blessings, both big and small, and find fulfillment in the present moment, rather than constantly striving for more.

The importance of abundance cannot be overstated. Embracing abundance allows us to shift our perspective, attract positive experiences, nurture fulfilling relationships, feed our bodies with bountiful and nutritious food, and cultivate a deep sense of gratitude and contentment.

It is a mindset that empowers us to tap into our true potential; manifest our dreams; and create a life of joy, fulfillment, and prosperity. By embracing abundance, we unlock the power to live a life of unlimited possibilities.

CHAPTER 2

THE CONNECTION BETWEEN AN ABUNDANT MINDSET AND FOOD

ave you ever considered the relationship between what you eat and your inner abundance?

It's an often-overlooked connection. I certainly didn't think about it when I restricted myself to a minimal food intake, obsessed over calories, and constantly worried about my body fat percentage. I believed that being extremely thin would make me feel abundant, but I couldn't have been more wrong. My body suffered from various issues like pulled groins, shin splints, and muscle tears due to a lack of nutrients. At that time, seeking external validation mattered more to me than providing my body energy to exercise twice a day. Yes, I said twice a day. My body fat was unhealthy at 9 percent when I was fifty, but that still wasn't good enough. When would it ever be enough? I shudder to think how scarce I was feeling back then. It's astonishing how our eating habits can reflect our internal state of scarcity.

What we eat significantly impacts how we feel and what we attract into our lives. The quality of food we consume can influence the energy stored within us. Remember, our feelings act as magnets that attract experiences from the universe. Therefore, food plays a crucial role in transitioning from a state of lack to one of abundance. If we've shifted our mindset and connected with our highest selves but continue to feed our bodies processed junk, we hinder our ability to manifest what we desire. Achieving alignment between mind, body, and spirit is essential to becoming an open and receptive channel.

Food is not merely sustenance; it is an entire experience. Who are you in the act of eating? Are you fully present in your body before savoring that first delightful bite? Are you taking a moment to appreciate the vibrant colors, varied textures, and nourishing properties of the food you consume? Are you present for those enjoying your meal with you? What kind of conversations are you making? Are you noticing your surrounding environment and enjoying your view? Did you express gratitude to the people who created your meal? In my perspective, true abundance is found when we become aware and fully engaged in the quality of our eating experiences.

Eating from an abundant plate goes beyond mindlessly consuming food while multitasking on a conference call or in the car before picking up your children. It is not about meticulously counting every calorie or denying yourself the pleasure of dessert. Embracing abundance means cultivating a different relationship with food. It means allowing food to become a part of you, relishing every mouthful.

I want to think back to the old scarce me who was counting every calorie and restricting the pleasure of eating food. I vividly recall how my relationship with food was deeply unhealthy due to the unresolved traumas of my childhood. I allowed myself to have an unhealthy self-image. I deprived myself of the joys of nourishment, believing I was unworthy. When I meticulously counted every calorie, I convinced myself I would only be loved if I achieved a perfect body—whatever that means! I judged my body mercilessly, even if it needed to gain weight. My body became the sole reflection of my self-worth. I exercised excessively, attempting to burn off every calorie I consumed. Pleasure was absent, and my plate was far from abundant. Eating became a mere necessity, devoid of enjoyment. The scarcity mindset that plagued me for most of my life manifested in the limited food choices and faith I had in my purpose and goals.

Now, through the process of healing my mindset, I have redefined my relationship with food. I have learned to embrace abundance and appreciate the nourishment it provides, both physically and emotionally.

In sharing my journey and the insights I have gained, I hope to inspire you to develop a healthier and more abundant relationship with food and understand that food can be a delightful way to heal every cell of your magnificent body. Now I encounter food as an experience, not just a necessity. Food and the experience of it is filled with joy and pleasure. I indulge all my senses in the experience.

In this book, you will find not just a rich tapestry of my life stories and food recipes but also mindset and life recipes. I wanted to create a holistic experience that goes beyond the realm of cooking and delves into the depths of personal transformation. Throughout my sixty—or what I say is "sex-ty"—years of life, I have transformed in a remarkable journey from a scarcity mindset to embracing magnificent abundance. What follows in these pages is a culmination of the lessons I have learned, the challenges I have faced, and the growth I have experienced along the way. Woven into these pages are captivating life stories that reflect the evolution of my mindset. From moments of doubt and limitation to profound moments of realization and expansion, these stories serve as a testament to the power of shifting perspective and embracing abundance in every aspect of life. Just as a well-crafted recipe requires the right ingredients and techniques, the same holds true for cultivating a mindset and life filled with abundance. You will discover the ingredients of self-love, gratitude, and mindfulness, along with the techniques to nurture and cultivate these qualities within yourself. Through the power of storytelling, I aim to inspire and empower you to embark on your own transformative journey. Whether you are seeking to overcome limiting beliefs, improve your relationship with food, or simply cultivate a more fulfilling and abundant life, the insights shared within these pages will guide you toward a path of growth and self-discovery. So, immerse yourself in these pages, savor the nourishing recipes, and allow the stories to ignite a spark of possibility within you. Together, let us embark on a journey from scarcity to magnificent abundance and create a life that is truly fulfilling and abundant in every sense.

Here are some of my favorite ways to expand your experience with food—abundantly, of course!

- Checking in with your emotions before eating and not eating until your body has connected to the parasympathetic nervous system, which allows rest and relaxation. This is the best way to digest.

- Pausing before eating and sending loving kindness to all those people who planted, harvested, made, and served the food to you. Like a prayer—but bigger.

- Break out the good china and enjoy your most abundant plate. No paper or plastic plates allowed.

- Chewing twenty-five times before you swallow. Break your food down so your body can break it down easier.

YOUR ABUNDANT AND SACRED PLATE STARTS IN YOUR KITCHEN

How can you infuse your kitchen with intention, mindfulness, and a sense of gratitude for the abundance it holds?

Clear and clean: Start by decluttering your kitchen and creating a clean, organized space. Remove unnecessary items and keep only the essentials. Clearing the physical space helps create a sense of openness and clarity.

Set an intention: Before you start cooking or preparing food, set an intention for your kitchen. This could be a simple affirmation or prayer expressing gratitude for the abundance of food and nourishment that will be created in the space.

Create a sacred altar: Dedicate a small area in your kitchen as a sacred altar. This can be a shelf or a designated spot on your countertop. Decorate it with items that hold personal significance, such as crystals, candles, or symbols of abundance and spirituality.

Incorporate natural elements: Bring elements of nature into your kitchen to enhance the sacredness. Bring in fresh flowers or potted plants to add life and vibrancy. Use natural materials like wooden utensils or bamboo cutting boards to connect with the earth.

Mindful food preparation: Approach food preparation with mindfulness and gratitude. Take the time to appreciate the ingredients, their origins, and the energy they provide. Engage all your senses while cooking, savoring the aromas, colors, and textures of the food. As we shift our inner vibrations, even the clothes we wear can reflect who we aspire to be or how we feel in the present moment.

Bless your food: Before eating, take a moment to bless your food. You can do this silently or with a prayer, expressing gratitude for the nourishment and abundance it provides. This practice helps cultivate a deeper connection to the food and the act of eating.

Share and connect: Make your kitchen a space for connection and sharing. Invite loved ones to join you in cooking or enjoying a meal together. Nourish your body, relationships, and sense of community.

Creating a sacred and abundant kitchen is a personal journey. Feel free to adapt these steps based on your own beliefs and preferences.

CHAPTER 3

THE ENERGY THAT WE HOLD

I want to transition here from the exploration of food's connection to abundance, to a journey into the depths of our being, focusing on the intricate relationship between the seven energy centers in the body, or chakras. They can affect the abundance we experience in our lives. Just as the nourishment we derive from food sustains our physical bodies, the energy coursing through our chakras nourishes our souls, shaping our experiences and perceptions in profound ways. When we have experienced any type of trauma from our childhood, we hold this energy in our energy centers, and if that energy or trauma is unhealed, it will continue to plague our energetic journey.

Each of our seven chakras, from the foundational root to the expansive crown, serves as a vital energy center, influencing various aspects of our existence. As we delve into the vibrational frequencies of these chakras, we uncover the subtle nuances of energy flow that dictate our sense of abundance or scarcity.

It is important to understand not only the individual roles of each chakra but also how they interact and intertwine to create our overall energetic feeling. By delving into the ways in which we hold and manage the energy within these centers, we gain insight into the patterns and beliefs that shape our experiences of abundance.

Through this deeper understanding, we empower ourselves to align our chakras with the frequencies of abundance, fostering a harmonious flow of energy that allows prosperity to flow effortlessly into our lives. Join me in unraveling the mysteries of our energy centers and unlocking the keys to manifesting greater abundance and fulfillment. It begins right here.

There are seven energy centers within our bodies that impact our overall well-being. Whether you follow the Hindu tradition of seven chakras or the Buddhist belief in five, we all possess these energy centers. From the root chakra to the crown chakra, each one represents a different aspect of our being. These chakras can vibrate either scarcity or abundance based on our internal dialogue.

Healing these seven chakras is a journey toward abundance. Our chakras store either abundant or scarce energy, depending on our trauma experiences, thoughts, and emotions. The stories we tell ourselves from childhood can influence our energetic frequency and determine our receptiveness to manifestation. Addressing and healing our chakras is crucial for shifting our inner frequency and attracting positive experiences. Blocked or imbalanced chakras can lead to physical discomfort, illness, or emotional disturbances. By recognizing and working on these energy centers, we can pave the way for a more abundant and harmonious life.

Incorporating healing foods that align with the colors of each chakra can enhance the energetic balance within us. Drawing from approaches like Ayurvedic medicine and Reiki, the connection between food and chakras becomes evident. By nourishing ourselves with foods that correspond to each energy center, we can restore balance and vitality. This holistic approach focuses on utilizing the natural colors of food for chakra healing purposes.

We can be transformed by the practice of mindful eating and understanding the relationship between food and our energy centers. By consciously choosing foods that support each chakra and noting how they affect our well-being, we can embark on a journey toward inner abundance and holistic healing.

In the intricate tapestry of our lives, the stories we habitually recount from our formative years yield significant influence over our frequency to manifest what we seek. These narratives, etched into the very fabric of our being since childhood, serve as the bedrock to which self-perceptions are built. Yet, beneath the surface of conscious awareness lies a network of energy centers, each acting as a repository for the beliefs we hold about ourselves.

Picture these chakras as the storerooms of our psyche in which every thought we harbor creates a ripple effect, resonating through our emotional landscape and imprinting the energetic fabric of our existence. It's a delicate dance between our thoughts that sculpt the contours of our emotional frequency, giving rise to a symphony of sensations that vibrate through every fiber and cell of our being.

Consider, for instance, the root chakra, often defined as the sturdy foundation upon which the structure of our existence stands. When this foundational energy center is infused with feelings of scarcity or insecurity, it sets the stage for a ripple effect that reverberates throughout our soul. Sometimes, we turn to food as a temporary refuge, hoping it will provide relief from the turmoil within us. And so, the intricate connection between our thoughts, emotions, and dietary choices becomes increasingly apparent. Our thoughts give rise to emotions, which, in turn, shape the energetic currents that flow within us. The emotions we carry are closely tied to the foods we crave, forming a cycle in which our eating habits affect our emotions, and vice versa. But what happens when these emotional currents encounter obstacles or disturbances? Much like a river obstructed by debris, our energetic flow becomes impeded, stifling the natural rhythm of abundance that courses through us. The traumas we carry, like stones in our riverbed, create eddies and whirlpools that distort the flow of energy, leading to a state of dis-ease within us.

Enter the healing power of intentional eating—an ancient practice that seeks to realign our energetic centers with the vibrational frequencies of abundance. By nourishing ourselves with foods that resonate with the colors associated with each chakra, we initiate a process of energetic recalibration, restoring harmony to our inner landscape.

Imagine a journey wherein the hues of crimson tomatoes and vibrant beets serve as the palette with which we paint our root chakra, infusing it with a sense of groundedness and stability. With each mindful bite, we reclaim our sovereignty over our energetic well-being, forging a deeper connection with the nourishing energies of the earth.

Holistic healing extends beyond the realm of dietary choices alone. It beckons us to explore the intricate web of emotions that lie at the heart of our being, inviting us to embark on a journey of self-discovery and self-transformation and returning us to our birthright of abundance. As we cultivate awareness around our emotional triggers and patterns of behavior, we gain insight into the deeper currents that shape our lived experience.

In this journey of self-exploration, every meal becomes a sacred ritual—a communion between body, mind, and spirit. We pause to savor the flavors, to acknowledge the emotions that arise within us, and to reconnect with the innate wisdom of our being. With each mindful bite, we affirm our commitment to self-nourishment, to the cultivation of abundance in all its forms.

And so, as we connect to the winding paths of our inner landscape, remember that the power to heal lies within us. By honoring the wisdom of our bodies, by nurturing ourselves with intention, by becoming aware of how we align our thoughts with our intention, we can unlock the gates to a life filled with boundless abundance and vitality.

 Root Chakra: Security, Survival

 Sacral Chakra: Sensuality, Creativity

 Solar Plexus Chakra: Confidence, Personal Power

 Heart Chakra: Compassion, Love

 Throat Chakra: Truth, Communication

 Third Eye Chakra: Insight, Intuition

 Crown Chakra: Enlightenment, Spirituality

PART II

THE
ENERGY
CENTERS

CHAPTER 4

THE ROOT CAUSE

ROOT CHAKRA

Our core, who we truly are at our essence, is deeply connected in the root chakra, the very foundation of our energetic being. This sacred space holds the memories of our past hurts and the masks we've worn, crafted from misunderstandings about ourselves. It holds beliefs created by others' unhealed energy from their pasts. According to scientific research, we energetically hold onto three generations of unhealed trauma.[1] Do you notice that you have taken on patterns and behaviors from your family of origin?

Like the sturdy cornerstone of a house, this chakra supports the rest of our energy system. When it's thrown off balance, it disrupts the flow of energy throughout our entire being, leading to disharmony, scarcity, and disempowerment. Within each of us lies an intricate network of energy centers, woven with the threads of our personal stories and experiences. As we navigate life, we intertwine with these narratives, too often embodying the energies that hinder our true potential. By delving into these energetic realms, we can begin to unravel the layers of conditioning and rediscover the boundless essence of our authentic selves.

How My Seed Was Planted

When I walked into the kitchen, the energy was frantic.

The night before had been typical for me as a teen—more late hours out drinking with my friends. Those local hangouts with the familiar smell of stale beer didn't seem to ever get old. They were places of laughter and connection to my friends. But this morning felt different. My mother was already dressed in her tidy jean skirt and her pink button-down shirt neatly tucked behind the leather belt she had bought at the local store in West Chester, Pennsylvania. Normally, she would be in her bedroom eating poached eggs on toast with a

---

1 https://sequencing.com/blog/post/what-ancestral-lineage-healing

cup of coffee and *The Christian Science Monitor* folded neatly beside her at this time. This was her routine for self-care and solitude before her busy day ahead.

That morning, the dishes were put away, the floor was swept, and the whole house smelled fresh and clean, like a hospital. My mom had even created one of her lavish floral arrangements. She would create these masterpieces whenever someone important was coming home or when we would throw a dinner party. My mother was a floral arranging extraordinaire! I remember her taking long walks in the fields that surrounded our country home with the two family dogs following faithfully at her heels. She would return with her arms full of foliage, tree branches, and colorful wildflowers that grew on the banks of the little stream surrounding our stone home. My grandmother's beautiful copper kettle with Chinese characters down the side became the perfect vessel for her magnificent arrangements.

This was not any day. This was a day of extreme importance. Charlotte, my sister, was coming for a visit from New York, and she was bringing home her new boyfriend. And this wasn't just any boyfriend. He was a wealthy art gallery owner from the Upper West Side of Manhattan. He drove a bright blue Rolls Royce—the car was so large that it struggled to turn into our narrow country driveway, almost hitting the white mailbox that my dad had just assembled. Each morning during his stay, we woke to the endless humming noise of his blow dryer coming from the downstairs bathroom with the fancy guest towels. His shoulder-length hair was slicked back, and his crisp white shirt matched perfectly with his dark-blue cashmere blazer. He was perfect—not a hair out of place as he waltzed into the kitchen to be fussed over.

That morning, I was dressed in my new blue overalls I had just purchased from our local thrift shop. I found them in a rack jammed with other cheap shirts and pants. The smell inside of the store was damp with a tinge of body odor, as if someone had just come inside from a heavy workout. I shopped there not because it was trendy but because it reflected how I felt about myself. This was where I felt comfortable and where my inner abundance and worth were aligned. Charlotte would not be wearing overalls or anything that didn't have a designer tag from Dior or Chanel. Her identity seemed to be wrapped in designer clothes and expensive labels.

The distribution of what was given to me versus what was given to my sister was completely out of balance when we grew up. I don't remember

exactly what the state of my family's finances was, but I didn't understand why my sister was given such abundance and I was not.

I want to make something clear. Perhaps there are some of you who may be rolling their eyes about my life and my story of scarcity. This was my interpretation as a child. I always had food on the table, clothes on my back, horses to ride. I had a certain degree of privilege. Many people may have suffered with no food or weren't even able to afford the basics to survive. But pain is pain; trauma is trauma. There is no higher level of either. To a child, the trauma, neglect, and how they live is an interpretation, a lived experience. My intention is not to compare my life to others who physically suffered but to help you understand why I developed this idea of my worth—the difference in how my sister and I were treated by our parents. I also want to note that there was nothing bad about my sister, either. She was, and is, a very kind and loving woman who has done amazing things in her life. This voice that is speaking here is the voice of my younger self. I felt terrible, and I began to sow the seeds of inner scarcity. This was my wound. This was the seed that I began to water that bloomed into the fruits in my adulthood.

Another interpretation or unbalanced alignment took place on a trip with my mother to buy me a pair of riding boots; even being able to buy riding boots, I understand, was a privilege. My boots were getting too small, so it was time for a new pair. Just weeks before, I had witnessed Charlotte unveiling a very large box with a postmark from Sweden. Her custom-made black riding boots had arrived. It was a big day for the family to watch her unveil these expensive boots. When the large white box emblazoned with an ostentatious logo finally arrived from overseas, the crisp, black tissue paper that was perfectly creased covered this new abundant purchase. The smell of expensive leather wafted into the air.

That familiar feeling of unworthiness bubbled up inside of me. I realized yet again I didn't deserve what my sister was experiencing. I was to be grateful for the boots that made my calves scream in discomfort. I had to be grateful for the boots with the cracks down the side and the worn-down heel on the left foot. I was to be grateful for what was given to me, even when I wanted to have what my sister was given. The pain from the boots was not as bad as the pain I felt from not being good enough to receive what my sister was receiving. This is what I told myself and identified with. What I wish I had known was there was nothing wrong with me. My seed was just different from hers. I learned from a young age that I had to accept what was given to me, not speak up or ask for what I wanted.

When I began to examine my misaligned energy of inner scarcity, the seed of my existence was revealed. It was like lifting a heavy rock from a riverbed to reveal the treasures underneath. The treasure in all of us is under the stories we tell ourselves. We are all abundant. It is our birthright. My seed created the belief of my unworthiness. We all have one that grows throughout our lives. I lived believing that abundance was not my birthright. I kept myself small and unnoticed. That experience in my youth was watered until adulthood. I watched others succeed. I yearned for something more. I compared myself to others who were living a life that I wanted, that was not available for me—only to my sister.

When I began my inner transformation, my thoughts, actions, and beliefs ascended to a life I have always only dreamed about. The quieter the old stories became, the more the treasures were revealed.

I am abundant now. I will allow myself to live in what I used to compare myself to.

Your Mind Is a Garden, Your Thoughts Are the Seeds

You can grow flowers or you can grow weeds. But sometimes we don't know which are flowers and which are weeds. In a single day, we think over seventy thousand thoughts. It's no wonder we can't tell the difference between the two. With a quiet mind we can reveal what we want to harvest.

There are positive energy cords that connect individuals to one another for the mutual benefit of both parties. These cords exist in relationships between lovers, parents and children, siblings, close friends, long-term coworkers, and anyone with whom you might feel a deep and positive connection.

Just as there are positive energy cords, there are also negative cords of attachment. These cords do not feed you positive and loving energy but rather take it away from you. When there is a negative cord, it will siphon your energy and give it to the individual on the other end of the cord.

Pulling the Weeds

Earlier, I talked about the practice of energy cord-cutting, which is all about releasing the burdens of the past. It's about letting go of anything that no longer serves us or aligns with our truth. Using visualization, we can energetically release the grip that our past has on us. It's a personal process, and what works for one person may not work for another. I invite you to keep practicing energy cord-cutting as many times as you need.

I found myself at a point where I didn't fully grasp what needed to change for me to truly transform my life. The feelings of scarcity, unworthiness, and inadequacy had become like a second skin to me—comfortable but outdated. It was time to shed that old identity and embrace something new.

My healing journey began by tuning into the energy within myself, tapping into the abundant vitality that resides in us all. It's about rediscovering our true essence and taking back our personal power.

Scarce Root

A scarce root chakra holds instability and insecurity.

Abundant Root

An abundant root chakra energy holds groundedness, stability, and belonging.

LIFE RECIPE AFFIRMATION: ROOT

"I am *rooted.*

I am *grounded.*

I am *secure."*

Reflect

How do you connect with your physical body and the earth to cultivate a stronger sense of belonging and safety?

Listen

The frequencies in music resonate with the root chakra, our fundamental energy center, which normally gets blocked by fear, anxiety, worry. This soundtrack promotes the healing of root chakra, removing all these blocks and boosting energy and positivity. Listen to this while preparing your meal or when you retire for the evening and transition to an abundant sleep.

Eat

Naturally red foods
Red apples
Tomatoes
Red bell peppers
Beets
Strawberries and other red berries
Watermelon
Cherries
Red grapes
Pomegranates
Cranberries
Red cabbage
Red meat, if it aligns with your diet and is consumed
in moderation
Grounding spices such as pepper, cumin, and paprika

Earthy, grounding foods
Mushrooms
Lentils
Quinoa
Whole grain breads and pastas
Potatoes
Kale
Wild rice
Brussels sprouts

Foods high in iron
Spinach
Tofu
Chickpeas
Pumpkin seeds
Dark chocolate

Root Rejuvenator Smoothie

INGREDIENTS

1 raw beet, red—some of you might be saying, "Yuck, I don't like beets."
Try it, but you can use other red vegetables or fruit if you can't stomach it.

1 handful of fresh or frozen strawberries—I always like them to be fresh!

1 handful of fresh or frozen raspberries

1 red apple, cut into pieces

A splash of almond, oat, or coconut milk—no dairy here, thank you!

A splash of organic orange or tangerine juice–you (or your partner) can freshly squeeze your juice!

HOW TO ENJOY

Mix everything together in your favorite blender.

Love Note

While blending, you can do a little dance!

Beet Bliss Hummus

INGREDIENTS

1 can of organic canned chickpeas

2 tablespoons of organic unsalted tahini—organic is best

1/3 cup of extra virgin olive oil

2 lemons

2 tablespoons of grated ginger

2 tablespoons of minced garlic

Salt

Love Note

Best eaten with cut red peppers, radishes, or green peppers.

HOW TO ENJOY

- Drain the chickpeas but save the liquid and set it aside. Soak the chickpeas in water for at least an hour. Then drain the water.

- Mix the chickpeas in a food processor until they are the consistency you like—I like mine smooth.

- Add 1/4 cup of the saved liquid—you decide if you want to add more.

- Add the organic unsalted tahini, extra virgin olive oil, the juice and zest from both lemons, the grated ginger, and the minced garlic.

- Add salt to taste.

- Mix everything in your food processor until blended.

- Chill the mixture in the fridge before eating.

For color variations, add any of the following:
- 1 raw red beet, minced

- 1 1/2 teaspoons of smoked paprika

- 3 cut and peeled yellow or orange carrots for your sacral and solar plexus variation

- 2 minced jalapeños, lime juice, and the zest of 2 limes for your spicy heart chakra variation

Wear

The energetic expression is rooted in feminine power; it is lighthearted, secure, and spiritual. By embracing the properties of the root color into your daily style, you will begin to create the grounded energy you wish to embody on the inside. It's an easy way to start training your mind to receive more abundance in this area of your life.

Accessorize with the color red, beaded, or hand-sewn materials, organically dyed fabrics, toe or ankle accessories, and select heirloom jewelry pieces as your anchors.

Decorate

The use of vibrant and deep red florals on your dinner table will naturally create a warm and comforting environment. Choose to share family-style for an extra special treat for your inner child to enjoy.

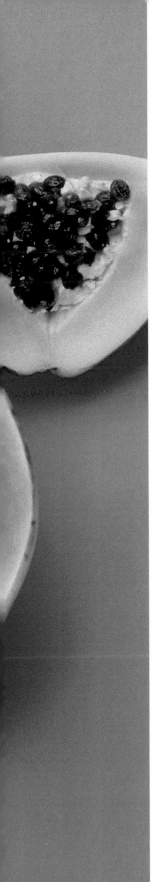

CHAPTER 5

YOUR SEXY SACRAL

SACRAL CHAKRA

Navigating the complexities of abundance and the sacral chakra often involves confronting moments of profound vulnerability and pain. In my own journey, this truth became starkly apparent during a fateful trip to Paris—a city renowned for its romance and allure, yet concealing shadows of my own internal turmoil. It was here amidst the cobblestone streets that I found myself caught in a web of deception and violation that shaped my thirty-two years of marriage. The memory is etched in my mind with painful clarity—a day in my nineteenth year filled with betrayal, as the innocence of my youth was shattered by the callous actions of another.

That memory? It was like a dam blocking the flow of my sacral chakra. That vital energy center, the source of my creativity, passion, and sexuality, was just . . . stuck. And I knew I had to do something about it. I had to break through that blockage, unleash the power within me.

So, I delved deep into myself, into the very core of my being where that memory was dormant. It was like excavating ancient ruins, each layer holding fragments of my past, of my struggles and fears. But I was determined to set myself free. As I uncovered that memory, I felt the weight of it pressing down on me, stifling my desires and my ability to truly connect with men on a deep, intimate level. It was like trying to breathe underwater—suffocating, constraining. I refused to let the scarcity of it hold me back any longer. With each breath, each moment of introspection, I chipped away at that dam, allowing the waters of my sacral chakra to flow freely once more.

And as I released that pent-up energy, that creative force within me, I felt alive in a way I hadn't in years. It was like the colors of the world were suddenly brighter, more vibrant. I was tapping into something primal, something sacred within myself.

But it wasn't enough to just break through that blockage. I knew I had to go further. I had to rewrite the script, to transform that memory from a burden into a source of strength. So, armed with my newfound sense of liberation, I began to rewrite my story. With each word, each affirmation, I felt the chains of the past falling away, replaced by a sense of empowerment and freedom.

And as the energy of my sacral chakra flowed naturally once more, I felt a profound sense of connection—to myself, to others, to the universe itself. It was a reminder that we are all beings of immense power and potential, capable of transcending even the darkest of shadows.

The Blocked Story

In my twenties, before I met my husband, my relationships were not working out. I was unwilling to heal the baggage that I carried with me. Exposing it to anyone meant rejection and abandonment, so I covered it over with a confident, fake smile. I had convinced myself that I was going to be single for the rest of my life. I noticed I was feeling emotions that were foreign to me, and my potential suitors seemed to run in the opposite direction whenever these strange, unearthed emotions came to the surface. Those feelings churned inside me like a hurricane. The trauma and pain of rejection and insecurities from past relationships felt unmanageable sometimes.

There was even room for a deep trauma of sexual abuse that I experienced in Paris. I had left the security of my family home and ventured off to an unknown place of adventure. I was to stay in France for one year as an au pair, looking after two little boys in Toulouse. The mother was an artist who only spoke Dutch and French, as did her boys. My high school French failed to help me understand the daily dialect. I did, however, become fluent, especially after drinking the local red wine. I was allowed a month off from my caregiving duties for Floris and Peter. They were naughty little boys. They would hide on the top shelf of the wooden armoire, giggling hysterically when I couldn't find them. Their manners were impeccable when they sat at the dinner table. Madam would make sure of this by reaching across the table and clunking the tops of their heads with her metal spoon if they spoke out of turn or ate too fast.

I chose to go to Paris for my month off and stay with an elderly woman and her daughter. This was a great adventure, and I got to know Paris like it was my hometown. I welcomed the hustle and bustle of city energy. The countryside in Toulouse was quiet, and the only excitement on a given day were the farm trucks delivering rolls of golden hay to the local hungry cows.

Paris was filled with parties and freedom from any responsibilities. I can remember going to an intimate dinner party at a new friend's home. The host presented dinner to us in a small stewing pot. I was horrified as I opened the lid and saw a whole rabbit cut up in parts and smothered with Dijon mustard. Its head was looking straight up at me. I graciously declined this rather strange delicacy. During my time there, no one knew I was

an American, as I had acquired the French look as well as the language. My hairstyle back then was short, with a long swoosh of hair in the front. My favorite piece of clothing was a vintage fur collar I matched with everything. It even looked perfect with my brightly colored red lipstick.

Each day I would take out my map (no GPS in those days) and set a course around each arrondissement. With my small black leather backpack, a bottle of water, and a carefully chosen outfit from the local Parisian flea market, I would begin my trek at exactly nine o'clock, stopping only throughout the day for a quick coffee and bread. It was all I could afford on a limited salary. I would, of course, pretend to be in abundance of financial flow, as I gazed past the various French clothing and shoe boutiques.

About two weeks into my grand adventure—a day that began as all the others did, backpack, water, outfit, and the map—I would be changed forever. My young innocence would be damaged by a stranger who somehow lured me into an abandoned building and molested me in one of the bathroom stalls. It happened so fast that I didn't know how to react quickly enough. As I stood with my legs wide open, standing on top of the broken toilet seat with my newly purchased trousers at my ankles, I felt helpless as he jammed his grimy, disgusting hand in my vagina. I can remember his fingers feeling cold, and he asked me in his strong French accent if I liked it. I don't recall what I said to him, as he began unbuckling his own pants. When I finally found my inner power, I kicked him backward and ran down the winding cold stairway, past the broken windowpanes, and out through the heavy wooden door with a large antique brass doorknob. The cold air outside woke me up instantly as I began to run the labyrinth of unfamiliar streets. There was no one there to protect me. There was no one to tell this young girl that everything was going to be okay. I had to bury my fearful trauma deep within me.

I remember that horrible life-changing day as if it were yesterday, but telling anyone would be too embarrassing. *How could you have allowed someone to do that to you? Why didn't you stop him? What were you wearing?* You know, those questions that people immediately ask to blame the victim. So, I held this story within me and never told a soul until I began my awakening and feeling my feelings from the past, thirty years later. No one in my family knew anything about this story. I have only just revealed this trauma to my daughter recently.

How I Found Abundance Once More

Before the powerful therapy of eye movement desensitization and reprocessing, I found myself adrift in a sea of misplaced longing, chasing after shadows of affection in the arms of the wrong men. Each fleeting encounter served as a painful reminder of my wounded soul, echoing the deep-seated wounds festering within the depths of my sacral chakra. Yet, within this darkness, a flicker of resilience began to emerge—a whisper of inner strength urging me to confront the shadows of my past and reclaim the abundance dormant within.

Yet, with each disappointment and heartache, the seeds of self-doubt were further sown, taking root in the fertile soil of my psyche. I began to internalize the belief that my worth was contingent on the validation of others—you know, men. I could only feel beautiful and desirable if someone else deemed me so. And so, I embarked on a futile quest for external validation, clinging to fleeting moments of affirmation like a lifeline in a sea of uncertainty.

But the more I sought validation from the outside, the more elusive it became, leaving me trapped in a vicious cycle of self-loathing and despair. I found myself scrutinizing every flaw, every imperfection, as if they were evidence of my inherent unworthiness. The mirror became my harshest critic, reflecting a distorted image of myself—a body marred by shame and insecurity, a soul burdened by the weight of unmet expectations.

It was a painful reckoning, coming face-to-face with the wounds I had long tried to conceal. Yet, in the depths of my despair, I began to glimpse a flicker of hope—a glimmer of possibility that whispered of redemption and renewal. Slowly, I began to unravel the layers of self-doubt and shame that had encased my spirit, confronting the lies that had long held me captive.

In reclaiming my inner abundance and embracing my inherent worthiness, I embarked on a journey of self-love and acceptance—a journey guided not by the fleeting affirmations of others but by the radiant truth of my own inner beauty. It was a journey marked by moments of vulnerability and courage, as I learned to embrace my body as a sacred vessel of creativity, sexuality, and a source of boundless strength.

And as I stood before the mirror, no longer seeing flaws but rather a reflection of resilience and grace, I knew that true beauty could never be found in the fleeting glances of strangers or the empty promises of lovers. It resided within me all along, waiting to be discovered and celebrated—a testament to the transformative power of love, both within and without.

Following that traumatic experience in Paris, I found myself grappling with the aftermath—a tapestry of emotions woven from threads of fear, shame, and profound loss. It was as if the vibrant hues of my sacral chakra had been muted, eclipsed by the shadows of trauma that loomed over my spirit. Desperate to escape the echoes of my past, I sought solace in the arms of men who offered fleeting moments of distraction but little genuine connection. Each encounter left me feeling emptier than before, a hollow shell of the vibrant soul I once knew.

But amid the darkness, a glimmer of hope beckoned—a gentle reminder that true abundance resides not in external validation or fleeting pleasures but in the depths of my own being. Slowly, tentatively, I began to turn inward, embarking on a journey of healing and self-discovery. It was a process marked by moments of profound introspection and raw vulnerability, as I confronted the wounds that lie buried within the recesses of my psyche.

As I connected deeper to the authenticity of my own consciousness, I unearthed a reservoir of untapped potential—a wellspring of creativity, passion, and resilience that lie dormant within me. With each step forward on my healing journey, the colors of my sacral chakra began to bloom once more. My life had a newfound sense of vitality and purpose.

In reclaiming my power and embracing my inherent worthiness, I discovered a profound truth—that true abundance begins from within. It is not measured by external trappings of success or fleeting moments of pleasure but by the depth of love and compassion we hold for ourselves. I knew that the journey ahead would be filled with challenges and triumphs, but that, ultimately, the greatest abundance of all awaited me—a life lived authentically in alignment with the radiant truth of my own soul.

Scarce Sacral

Scarce sacral chakra energy holds loneliness, low libido, a lack of creative inspiration, and isolation.

Abundant Sacral

Abundant sacral chakra energy holds enhanced creative expression, improved sexual intimacy, passion, and increased intuition.

LIFE RECIPE AFFIRMATION: SACRAL

"I am *worthy. I am joyful. I am creative.*"

Reflect

What steps can you take to nurture your creativity and embrace the flow of your emotions more freely?

Listen

When balancing your sacral, listening to 432 hertz will help connect you to the universe; remove guilt, shame, and dependence; balance emotions; let go of draining negative emotions; and remove emotional blockages.

Eat

Naturally orange foods
- Carrots
- Sweet potatoes
- Oranges
- Pumpkins
- Apricots
- Mangoes
- Papayas
- Cantaloupes
- Winter squashes such as butternut, acorn, and spaghetti

Foods that support reproductive health
- Leafy greens
- Avocado
- Salmon
- Walnuts
- Eggs
- Beans and lentils
- Greek yogurt
- Citrus fruits

Pleasurable treats
- Dark chocolate
- A delicious cocktail
- Seasonal fruits
- A cup of tea or coffee
- Chia seed pudding
- Baked apples or peaches
- Frozen yogurt
- Foods with warming spices such as nutmeg, cinnamon and allspice
- Anything else that gives you a sense of delight

Golden Glow Butternut Squash Soup

INGREDIENTS

1 tablespoon avocado oil

1 golden butternut squash

3 sweet potatoes, cubed—cook for 1 minute
   in microwave so the sweet potato is softer

1 red onion, chopped

1 tablespoon garlic, chopped—you can
   microwave or roast for even more
   abundant flavor

2 teaspoons turmeric—any will do, but I love
   my Egyptian turmeric!

2 teaspoons fresh ginger, chopped—
   be generous!

6 cups vegetable broth—organic, of course!

Salt and pepper to taste

HOW TO ENJOY

1. In a large saucepan over medium-high
   heat, add oil and the onion. Cook the
   onion for 5 minutes.

2. Add the rest of the ingredients,
   reduce heat, and simmer for 25
   minutes. You can dance while it's
   cooking!

3. With a hand blender, purée the
   mixture until you have a smooth
   texture. Love this part!

4. Serve hot with the garnish of your
   choice.

Enjoy!
So good!

Passion Papaya Delight—Sacral Smoothie

INGREDIENTS

1/2 cup of fresh papaya—the color and taste are fabulous! Don't worry about the smell!

1 cup of fresh pineapple—don't be fooled by the bigger ones! Size here doesn't mean better!

1 fresh or frozen banana—your choice! You can always add ice to make it colder!

A pinch of turmeric—or more! It is my favorite spice! It is a great anti-inflammatory!

1 orange, juiced, or 1/4 cup of organic orange or tangerine juice

HOW TO ENJOY

Combine all ingredients into a blender and blend until smooth.

Love Note

Remember to use a beautiful glass.
Plastic not allowed!

Sacral Coconut Golden Milk

INGREDIENTS

2 cups of unsweetened coconut milk (or milk of your choice)—coconut is better here!

1 tablespoon of grated fresh ginger (or 1 teaspoon of ground ginger)—be generous here; ginger is so good for your digestion.

1 tablespoon of grated fresh turmeric (or 1 teaspoon of ground turmeric)

1/2-inch piece cinnamon (or 1/2 teaspoon of ground cinnamon)—I like to use the stick to stir the goldenness!

1 teaspoon of honey—try and find it from your local farmers market!

HOW TO ENJOY

1. Place all ingredients in a small pot or saucepan and bring to a gentle boil.

2. Simmer for 10 minutes or so. Keep covered, stir occasionally.

3. Remove from heat and strain. Decant into two mugs to serve.

Love Note

My favorite cups for this recipe are heart-shaped!

Wear

The energetic expression is sophisticated elegance, sensuality, and spiritual humor. By embracing the properties of the sacral color into your daily style, you will begin stimulating the creative energy you wish to embody on the inside. It's an easy way to start training your mind to receive more abundance in this area of your life.

Accessorize with the color orange, artistic patterns, specialty undergarments, silky-soft fabrics, and items that make you say, *"Damn, I feel incredible!"*

Decorate

Even candle light can be a source of the hue of orange. Whether with real candles or battery operated, illuminate your rooms in every dark corner with light.

CHAPTER 6

YOUR GUTSY GUT

SOLAR PLEXUS CHAKRA

The solar plexus, often regarded as our energetic center of personal power and will, plays a significant role in our experience of abundance. When our solar plexus is balanced and activated, we feel empowered, confident, and capable of manifesting our desires. It's the seat of our self-esteem, courage, and determination—the very qualities that propel us toward creating an abundant life.

Your Power Lies in Your Allowing

Allowing ourselves to experience abundance requires a sense of inner strength and self-assurance, which are attributes closely associated with the solar plexus. When this energy center is in harmony, we feel a deep sense of trust in ourselves and the universe, knowing that we have the power to shape our reality.

Moreover, the solar plexus governs our relationship with power—personal power and our ability to attract abundance. When this energy center is blocked or imbalanced, we may experience feelings of insecurity, self-doubt, or a lack of confidence, which can hinder our ability to manifest abundance.

By working on the solar plexus through practices such as meditation, visualization, breathwork, and affirmations, we can clear any blockages and activate this center, allowing the free flow of energy and empowering ourselves to embrace abundance fully.

Furthermore, the solar plexus is associated with the element of fire, symbolizing transformation and the drive to achieve our goals. When we stoke the flames of our inner fire, we ignite our passion and ambition, fueling our journey toward abundance.

In essence, nurturing and balancing the solar plexus is essential for cultivating the mindset and inner strength necessary to allow abundance into our lives fully. As we align our personal power with the flow of universal abundance, we create a harmonious relationship between our desires and the infinite possibilities available to us.

My Abundant Allowance

The water was calm that day when we lowered our bags into the wooden taxi boat. Antonio was impeccably dressed and looked as if he spent hours ironing his crisp, white shirt and the blue three-piece suit that he was wearing when we arrived at the port. I even noticed that his nametag sparkled in the bright Italian sunlight. Making sure we were safely seated in the bow of the boat, he untied the ropes from the jetty, turned on the engine, and slowly pulled out from the port. I felt relaxed even after our eight-hour flight from New York to Venice. I can never sleep on planes, and I find it annoying to see other passengers in a deep slumber. I usually only manage an hour of sleep, waking to neck pain and discomfort in my hips from trying to twist into a comfortable position.

Our water taxi driver was patiently waiting for us with the sign clearly written on the white board. He gathered our luggage and remarked, "You don't have to do anything from now on!" What? This certainly wasn't what I was used to!

We began the journey across the canal. The once calm waters began to get choppy the farther we motored across the canal. Inhaling, I wanted to take this all in! The water in the middle of the grand canal was full of activity—the vaporetti, private water taxis, barges delivering goods, police emergency boats, fire and ambulance services, and of course the traditional poled gondolas. I noticed the sunshine—an orange and yellow reflection on the stone buildings coming into view.

The hum of this city became livelier as we neared our hotel on the opposite side of the canal—the hustle of tourists walking to wait in line for their favorite museum exhibit; the souvenir vendors selling T-shirts of the *Mona Lisa*; the relaxing noise of the empty gondolas splashing in the water. We paused as our taxi carefully maneuvered around the black gondolas with red velvet seats and bunches of colorful plastic flowers tucked neatly in between the seats in the middle.

We finally headed into the canal where the front door of our hotel was ready to welcome us. With a slow turn of the boat and a loud roar of its engine, we drifted perfectly to the front entrance. We were greeted by the staff at Hotel Danieli, a renowned five-star luxury hotel a few steps away from Piazza San Marco. The rich, ornate, wooden doors welcomed us into the elegance of this fourteenth-century palace.

Yes, I said palace! I had never allowed myself to experience the abundance of such a place. As we walked to the reservation desk, I noticed the white marble floors and mahogany walls greeted us. I looked up and was transported back in time to the opulence and splendor of the Italian Renaissance.

This was a stark contrast to what I experienced in my thirty years of marriage. The last time I was looking up at a ceiling in a hotel, it looked different from the exquisite view of the Danieli.

I'm cringing right now writing this chapter! That familiar sensation of trying to not sound spoiled and privileged keeps bubbling up. That fear of being judged by someone who doesn't know me personally. It feels like the same sensation in my solar plexus I experienced throughout my childhood and adulthood. That reminder of those thoughts to not sound ungrateful for what has been given. *Be grateful, Sarah!* How did they know I wasn't? My intention is to show you that the feeling of scarcity can have an impact on what you think you deserve, what you allow yourself to experience, and how you speak up for yourself, especially because I was a stay-at-home mom. I assure you I have a reason to share this with you.

During my marriage, it became clear that I had held onto the scarce energy of my mother who didn't think that she deserved anything nice. She carried the ancestral energy from her three generations. I then carried the same energy and attracted the same type with my then-husband, John. He didn't think he deserved nice things, either. Extravagance was something foreign to him. When I met him in West Chester, Pennsylvania, his possessions were simple: a handmade black wooden bed; a sofa; one fork; one knife; and a large print photo of a naked Nastassja Kinski with a large python wrapped around her body. That's it. Nothing else.

My then-husband worked hard for our family and was the greatest provider to me and to our four children. He wore the same plaid shirt to work most of the week. The same dark-blue pants he would wash every other day. He had the same five pairs of blue socks carefully folded in the top drawer of his bureau. Nothing frivolous or flashy.

When we would travel, our hotel of choice was the Hampton Inn. I get it—traveling with six was expensive; but we had the money for better accommodations. We had plenty of money for occasional splurges, but we never used it that way. We stocked our bank account and saved every penny. That's what he was told by his parents. Don't spend. Save everything. I didn't ask for anything more. I didn't feel I deserved it. I was to be grateful for what was given to me. This was about my personal power to speak up and ask. I felt like I couldn't even discuss how the money was spent or if we should save every penny. This was my inner story. I was the girl who was given the boots that made her calves scream in pain. I couldn't ask for more.

I remember one vivid instance of my disempowerment when I was in Ohio. I was traveling with my four children on our way to one of my husband's car races. Here again was the confusion I felt with my family's finances. We would save every penny, and my husband would be the only one to decide how the money was spent. I thought, "He earns the money, so he can make the decisions about how to spend it." I said nothing when he wanted to own a race car team. That is expensive. He didn't have an issue purchasing race cars, but he had no interest in spending the money on anything that would have been luxurious. He encouraged me to spend money on schooling or something practical. I didn't, but when

I wanted to spend money on myself for something extravagant, I felt his disapproval and guilt for even wanting to.

When the kids and I were at his races, he would stay and sleep at the track with the team and make repairs to the car, so I would be alone with our children. On this night in Ohio, I had to find a particular hotel in the dark on my own with the children asleep in the back of the car. I was afraid for myself and my children, but I was also feeling the fear of not speaking up for myself. That night we all arrived at the hotel very late. It was in the middle of nowhere and seemed to date back to the early seventies. The reception desk was an outdoor window with bars, as if we were entering a jail cell. I had to tilt my head to the side to speak to the clerk. After I got the keys, we drove our car to the back to find the correct room number. As we entered, there was a strong stale smell that wafted in our faces. It smelled like the inside of a sweaty gym bag. "Quickly," I said to my kids, "open a window." The windows were locked shut, so we had to compromise and turn on the air conditioner that rattled when we turned the knob to high. I gathered my children to brush their teeth and use the toilet before climbing into bed. I noticed the shower head dangling from the wall; as I peeked behind the curtain, I saw shampoo and conditioner sitting on the edge of the tub with yellow water stains around the drain. The kids were so tired they climbed into bed and fell straight asleep. I did not. I was convinced there was a creature crawling in bed with me and kept turning on the light to see if my imagination was real. I never really slept.

I remember telling myself that same story. "Be grateful, Sarah. Don't say anything. John will think you are spoiled and entitled." I had heard those words before during one of our many heated arguments. "It must be nice," he would say. "You have no idea what it's like to be the breadwinner. You are so entitled and spoiled. You need to be more grateful."

I kept quiet, then said the hotel was great. We all slept really well.

Back to Italy

The view from the reception desk was exquisite. There were extravagant oil paintings with brushed gold frames. Orchids and exotic plants hung from the walls at each level of the stairs, cascading down like a beautiful green waterfall. Crushed red velvet carpeting led the way up the stairs to the fifth level of our awe-inspiring hotel. I had never experienced anything like this. Some rooms cost eight thousand dollars a night. Mostly movie stars and dignitaries stayed in these suites. My partner and I did not stay on that side of the hotel, but still our hotel room was spectacular! The large open-pane window looked out onto Piazza San Marco. Each morning at six, we were softly awakened by the clock tower in the church. Our bed had a canopy with a gold velvet bedspread. The sheets underneath were as soft as butter. I stood quietly for a moment and reflected on how far in my healing I had come. The idea of allowing myself such abundance was more than I could have imagined. I felt

uncomfortable when I pressed "Complete Purchase" a month earlier when I finally booked the trip. Those familiar limited stories were there wanting my attention and wanting me to believe that I really didn't deserve this room. I didn't deserve the chocolates left on the pillows or the complimentary champagne cooling on ice. We all deserve luxurious pleasure, and we don't deserve to feel guilty about it.

The next morning, we woke to the chiming of the Campanile di San Marco. We opened the window to the cool Italian air and could hear the quiet bustle of the morning streets beginning to stir. I could feel my stomach begin to churn, looking forward to the breakfast that was awaiting us on the third floor. This wasn't a breakfast of colorful cold cereal; this was a breakfast that looked like it was being laid out for a king and queen. The length of an entire wall was adorned with fifty different cheeses from around the world. Heaps of colorful fruit filled large, gold bowls. Croissants and thinly sliced breads were delicately arranged with butter, honey, and jam. The omelet station with your own personal chef; a bar of freshly squeezed juices; champagne and prosecco to mix for mimosas—I didn't know where to begin. The restaurant was on the third floor with a view of that grand canal that looked like a Renaissance painting. As I drank my orange and clementine mimosa, I could see the Doge's Palace. The boats were already making soft wakes in the water below. In that moment, I realized how much I had transformed myself and had reframed my value and inner worth. This was my new story that I was telling myself. This was my reframe. What I felt inside was being reflected on the outside.

The Allowing

Maybe your worth isn't wrapped in luxurious experiences like staying at a five-star hotel or traveling first class. My point here is about allowing. The allowing is the abundance. In my stories, the finances did not change. What did change was my perception of what I allowed myself to experience. So many of my clients who begin working with me don't even allow themselves to light a candle in the morning or luxuriate in a bubble bath. Self-care is abundant. Denying yourself the richness of life is scarcity. I remember my mom had beautiful china that was always stored in a cupboard. She would say, "They are too nice to use." So this beautiful china would sit on the shelf in her cottage collecting dust. Is it unhealed, limiting stories of our family that are setting that standard? I know that I held onto the unhealed stories of my mother.

Go Ahead

Light the candle. Use good china. Take that trip of a lifetime. Do something you've never done before. The idea here is to reevaluate your self-worth by taking tiny steps. This is how we elevate our energetic frequency and become the abundant reservoir to our most fulfilled life.

What do you believe is your worth?

Earlier, I explored a profound idea—that the seeds of our beliefs shape the landscape of our lives. These seeds are planted in the fertile soil of our childhood, nurtured by the stories we absorb from our family and surroundings. They grow into the narratives that guide our decisions, shape our relationships, and color our experiences.

At the heart of these narratives lies the concept of self-worth—a fundamental belief in our own value and deservingness of love. It's the foundation upon which our sense of identity and worthiness is built. When our self-worth is abundant, we navigate life with a sense of confidence and self-assurance. We're able to accept ourselves, flaws and all, and embrace the love and kindness that others offer us.

However, for many of us, self-worth can be a fragile thing, easily shaken by self-doubt and criticism. This fragility often stems from the stories we internalize as children—the messages that tell us we're not good enough, smart enough, or worthy of love. Over time, these beliefs become deeply ingrained, shaping how we see ourselves and interact with the world.

But here's the thing—self-worth is not set in stone. It's a fluid and malleable aspect of our being, influenced by our thoughts, beliefs, and experiences. By recognizing the origins of our self-doubt and challenging the negative narratives we've internalized, we can begin to rewrite our story. We must reclaim our inherent worthiness, acknowledge our strengths, and learn to love ourselves unconditionally.

This journey of self-empowerment is not always easy. It requires courage, self-reflection, and a willingness to confront our deepest fears and insecurities. But with each step we take, we move closer to a place of greater self-acceptance and inner peace. We learn to silence the critical voices that hold us back and embrace the truth of our own worthiness. And in doing so, we open ourselves up to a life filled with love, joy, and possibility.

Scarce Solar Plexus

Scarce solar plexus chakra energy holds low self-confidence and self-esteem, insecurity, and a need for confirmation from others.

Abundant Solar Plexus

Abundant solar plexus chakra energy holds high levels of self-esteem, inner strength, and resilience—the ability to easily make choices.

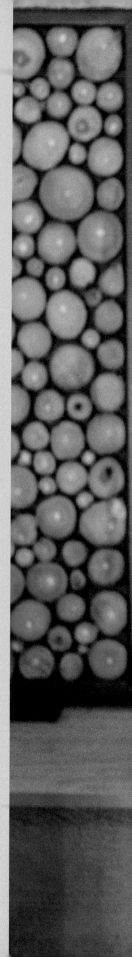

LIFE RECIPE AFFIRMATION: SOLAR PLEXUS

"I am *powerful*.

I am *enough*.

I am *abundant*."

Reflect

What actions can you take to step into your personal power and embrace your true potential?

Listen

Meditating on the solar plexus chakra helps uncover the real jewel we all are. It is also helpful in reducing stomach ulcers, irritable bowel syndrome pain, and keeps our digestive system healthy. So, the flow of energy in this chakra is important. Listening to the melodic vibration of Indian flute music for your solar plexus in the root note of E will resonate and energize this chakra, unblocking energy flow in the region.

Eat

Naturally yellow foods
Bananas
Lemons
Yellow bell peppers
Yellow squash
Eggs
Pineapples
Yellow lentils
Olive oil
Corn
Golden beets
Yellow watermelons
Yellow tomatoes
Yellow split peas
Foods containing golden spices such as turmeric, saffron, curry, and cardamom

Foods that aid in healthy digestion
Yogurt
Kimchi, sauerkraut, and other probiotic fermentations
Ginger
Kombucha
Fennel
Whole grains

Foods that make you feel energized
Green tea (or coffee or your tea of choice)
Honey
Balsamic vinegar
Citrus fruits
Fresh herbs
Chicken, fish, tofu, tempeh, and other lean proteins for sustained energy

Confidence Elixir Smoothie

INGREDIENTS

1 fresh or frozen banana—I always like it fresh!

1 mango, peeled

Juice of 1/2 a lemon—oh how I love lemons! They make me so happy!

1 inch of ginger root—indulge in ginger. It's so good for you!

1 inch of turmeric root

HOW TO ENJOY

- Put all ingredients into a blender and blend until smooth.

Love Note

Enjoy! Remember to drink from a beautiful glass! No plastic allowed here!

Cauliflower Power Soup

INGREDIENTS

6 cups of yellow cauliflower florets—did you know that cauliflower takes on the taste of whatever you cook it in?

3 cloves of garlic, minced—you could even roast the garlic or microwave it briefly to bring on the flavor

2 tablespoons of avocado oil

1/2 tablespoon of olive oil—if you can't go to Italy to get your olive oil, get organic extra virgin olive oil

1 teaspoon of turmeric or 1 turmeric root, peeled—organic if possible

1 teaspoon of ground cumin

1/8 teaspoon of crushed red pepper flakes—whatever your heat tolerance

1 large red onion or fennel bulb, minced—don't cry; wear your goggles!

3 cups of vegetable broth—organic here, please!

1/4 cup of full-fat coconut milk—shake to get all the lumps out

HOW TO ENJOY

- Preheat your oven to 450°F.

- In a large bowl, mix the cauliflower florets with minced garlic and 2 tablespoons of oil until well coated.

- Add turmeric, cumin, and red pepper flakes, and toss to coat evenly.

- Spread the cauliflower on a baking sheet in a single layer and bake for 25–30 minutes, until browned and tender. You'll know it's ready when the smell of garlic fills your kitchen.

- While the cauliflower is baking, heat the remaining teaspoon of oil in a large pot over medium heat. A cast iron pot works wonderfully for this.

- Add the chopped onion and cook for 2–3 minutes, until translucent.

- Once the cauliflower is finished baking, remove it from the oven. Reserve 1 cup of roasted cauliflower to top the soup.

- Add the remaining roasted cauliflower to the pot with the onion. Pour in the vegetable broth.

- Bring the mixture to a boil, then cover and cook over low heat for 15 minutes.

- Blend the soup to a smooth purée using an immersion blender or let it cool slightly and purée in batches with a regular blender.

- Serve the soup topped with the reserved cauliflower and a drizzle of coconut milk.

Love Note

*Enjoy your delicious homemade
cauliflower soup and eat from your
gorgeous china that you never use!*

Wear

The energetic expression is play-ful, confident, and powerful. By embracing the properties of the solar-plexus color into your life's daily style, you will begin to create the empowered energy you wish to embody on the inside. It's an easy way to start training your mind to receive more abundance in this area of your life.

Accessorize with the color yellow, blooming florals, sun symbols, blinging belt buckles, and choose golden or sparkling accents to truly shine.

Decorate

When we decorate, we can incorporate our authentic expression by shifting our solar plexus by, for example, adding an element of humor.

You can shake things up with cardio, or you can shake things up with humor! Get those belly laughs roaring!

I NEVER GO JOGGING,
IT MAKES ME SPILL MY MARTINI.

-GEORGE BURNS

CHAPTER 7

HELLO, HEART

HEART CHAKRA

The energetic center of our heart chakra that exists within all of us is incredibly important for healing and removing blockages.

At the core of our being, our essence is love. It is a universal desire for all people and animals to be loved and to experience love. Imagine a world in which we fully understand this concept and live with love in our hearts without any conscious effort. In such a world, there would be no wars, conflicts, broken marriages, abuse, or abandonment. Life would feel effortless and harmonious. However, the reality is that fear exists. We often perceive fear to be more powerful than love, and this perception creates challenges in our lives.

When we recognize that love is at the core of our being, we begin to realize that it is the driving force behind all our actions and emotions. When we live with love in our hearts, we approach every situation with compassion, empathy, and kindness. So, while fear may exist, and at times feel overwhelming, we must remember that love is always present within us. It is a choice we can make every day to prioritize love over fear, to act with love, and to cultivate a loving energy that radiates outward and impacts those around us.

By fully understanding and embodying the concept of love, we can create a ripple effect that spreads love, compassion, and harmony throughout the world. It all starts within our own hearts, as we tap into our energetic center and allow love to guide us toward a brighter, more loving existence.

Letting Go

The room that day felt cozy and safe, like it always did. I had visited this room many times with my family—at Christmas or at one of my children's birthday parties. Today was different. I knew it was time. It was time to let go of a place that gave me strength, faith, and hope when I felt sadness, uncertainty, and anger. I would sit quietly with my coffee in the mornings here, with the streams of warm sunlight shining through the windows. I would just sit and breathe in the air and take some time for myself to reflect each morning and meditate before the rush of my four children's school routines. The rich wood floors, the high vaulted ceiling, and the massive gold leaf mirror that hung over the fireplace added to the sense of familiarity and safety; but that morning I knew. It was time to go. Time to embark on a newness in my life. Time to face the fears that had embedded in my soul for fifty-seven years. It was time. I could feel it in my body. The answers I was searching for and the questions I kept asking myself were about to unfold on the other side of the leaving. I had to do something different. It had been way too long to not listen to my inner voice that was telling me I was going to be all right. I could make it on my own. I could handle my own finances and have a good relationship with money. I had ignored anything to do with money throughout my thirty years of marriage. I heard that same voice years earlier, but I didn't listen or do anything different.

As I sat and meditated that morning in my familiar and safe living room, there was a force within me this time to make my move. I called out to my husband to come and talk to me in my sacred space. He knew. We were at the end, and he could sense it in his soul, like me. We sat for quite a while together, tenderly listening to one another and gently touching each other's hands. We didn't want anything from one another. It was a time when we were just being present and listening to each other's words. Not trying to be right. Not trying to disagree. Just a place of deep listening. There was nothing to lose or gain in the end, just sadness that filled my body knowing the uncertainty of what would come next.

Weeks before, we had one of our monthly fights. Oh, how I remember the emotions that would swirl within me. The anger deep in my soul that would suddenly erupt with no place for the energy to go. He didn't want to hear it, nor did he know how to console it. We were so different. I welcomed any emotion that would bubble up. He avoided anything that felt uncomfortable; he would run to his safe refuge in the garage to tinker on one of his many projects. Cars were his thing. Anything with an engine seemed to be more relatable than his wife of thirty years.

The emotions that arose in our last fight were stronger than I had ever felt before. The catalyst for the fight is a long story—and doesn't really matter. What matters is the panic that scared me that night. As did the silence. The cruelty and fear that was being passed between us was not fair. He wouldn't speak to me as we drove down the dark and winding roads back to our home in Maryland. We had tried to go on an overnight trip to be alone finally at our beach home in Delaware. His way of controlling the discomfort of an emotional fight was to threaten to turn the car around and go home. And this time he did, only to remind me of the parent-child dynamic between us. The feeling of disempowerment consistently filled my inner being.

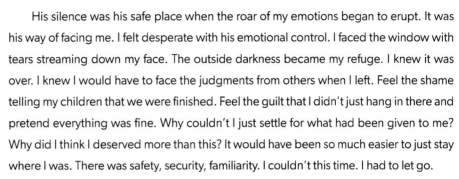

His silence was his safe place when the roar of my emotions began to erupt. It was his way of facing me. I felt desperate with his emotional control. I faced the window with tears streaming down my face. The outside darkness became my refuge. I knew it was over. I knew I would have to face the judgments from others when I left. Feel the shame telling my children that we were finished. Feel the guilt that I didn't just hang in there and pretend everything was fine. Why couldn't I just settle for what had been given to me? Why did I think I deserved more than this? It would have been so much easier to just stay where I was. There was safety, security, familiarity. I couldn't this time. I had to let go.

After we hugged one another, we decided to separate for two weeks. You know, take a baby step, so as not to feel overwhelmed and do nothing—a common practice among people who are trying to create a new habit. The plan was for me to move to our home in Delaware. He would stay at our family home in Maryland. We wanted to listen to our souls to see whether this was the right step for both of us. And it was. Three years later we are officially divorced. We signed on the line and ended what we thought would be a forever union. I have become a proud, divorced fifty-nine-year-old woman. This woman is not filled with shame that I did something wrong. She isn't filled with guilt that I've traumatized my grown children and that they would be scarred for life. No matter where she is or what she is doing, she will be there to support any pain that arises within them. She isn't full of regret that she did the wrong thing or should have just silenced the voice inside.

She has aligned with the woman that was screaming to be free and live this present life in the most abundant way. Never will I regret any part of my gorgeous marriage or be filled with resentment. We both did our best to show up to one another with what was modeled from our parents.

My life now has no familiarity to how I lived most of my life. No, I don't have little children under my feet, an ark full of animals to take care of, or anyone to put before me; but there could still be some sort of fear or excuse that I could use. But I'm not. I am taking chances, facing and feeling all my fears, creating a new and empowered relationship with investments and my finances. I have opened my heart wide with no regret to a new partnership with an amazing man. I am traveling the world, spreading my message to a larger audience, signing my books, writing more, and most importantly, loving myself in the deepest way that I can. No judgments here. No self-loathing or criticism ever again. I am reaping all the rewards from my healing. I am now living a life that I never thought possible. You can, too.

What We Witness

How we witness our parents behavior in their relationships is what we model in ours. What I can remember between my parents was not what I dreamed about experiencing. Back then I didn't know any better. Why is it that we model what we don't want? We tell ourselves that we will not behave like our parents, and when we are adults, we experience exactly that. It's energy. We witness the behavior that creates our thoughts. Our thoughts create the energy we hold in our bodies. That energy is what we then attract in our own behavior. It's that simple. I didn't know what I know now. I entered my own marriage without a model of what abundant love looked or felt like. I believe that this is the case for most relationships. This is why in the United States, between 35 and 50 percent of first marriages end in divorce, increasing to approximately 60 percent for second marriages and more than 70 percent for marriages after the second. This gives the US one of the highest divorce rates in the world. I knew I needed my parents to show me how to love, how to respect one another and grow gracefully together rather than apart. I wanted them to show me how to partner with respect and patience. I wanted to be shown how to have fun and laugh at the silliest of things. I wanted to see physical affection and a loving embrace. That was not what was mirrored to me. Instead, I learned how to be defensive. I learned how raising your voice was the only way to be heard. I learned that showing physical affection or showing emotion was a weakness—all coming from emotional scarcity.

For most of my marriage, something felt off. Something was misaligned within me, so my inner vibration attracted him. His family was similar to mine. That ungenuine facade of strength was covering inner emotional scarcity. We both witnessed the inability to show love and receive love. We both wanted to teach our children how to feel the most powerful and abundant energy of all—love. I can remember my husband telling me that his mother would never say "I love you" to her children. She believed children should know that their parents love them. Their parents should not have to tell them. What?

My mother was English, and my husband's mother was Dutch. Their ranking in social class gave them their sense of abundance. Being born with this social ranking was the gauge by which they felt abundant. Instead, the unresolved pain from their childhoods entered our sacred union. We did not know how to show love to one another in a way that would have bonded us together until the end. This was sad and frustrating for both of us. All marriages have their flaws and areas that shed light onto where our greatest fears lie. But what we both truly needed from one another was what we were unable to give. We both wanted to feel loved, to feel that magical emotion. But we didn't know how. We didn't know how to show affection. We didn't know how to raise each other up. What I know now is the closer we get to our core essence, which is the energy of love, the easier

it is to show love.

Back in 1990, my inner scarcity of safety and security was in full bloom. Someone to take care of me, be a financial provider, be loyal and faithful to me—that's exactly what was given to me in our thirty years together. Bless him. He wanted a wife that would give him the sense of family, take care of all the issues with the children, have the dinner cooked when he returned home from a hard day at work. Someone to fill what was not secured in his own childhood by his own mother. Living in South Africa for most of his life, he experienced the abandonment of his beloved home when apartheid was about to end. Their family had fifteen minutes in the middle of the night to gather any possesions and fly to the US with their sponsor. There was no time to bring any sentimental items that would have given him comfort. Everything was left behind.

I gave him what was missing within him. We both gave to one another what we both lacked. It was that inner emptiness that both of us were able to fill for one another.

Making Divorce an Abundant Experience

Whether you are divorcing or breaking a romantic or friend relationship, how we think about our circumstance has a big impact on what we experience. How would you react to an uncoupling of any relationship? Would you hold resentment, bitterness, or guilt? What would those emotions really do for you? The only person that it would affect is you. Resentment is like drinking poison and waiting for the other person to die. I promise you that avoiding a scarcity mindset will help you achieve a life full of energetic flow, happiness, and joy. The natural flow of abundant energy is a birthright. We all have it within us. If we bring fear, jealousy, revenge, guilt, or any low-vibration energy, we are living in a scarcity mindset. I was very fortunate to have my ex-husband feel the same way about our impending split as I did. He, too, wanted a positive outcome to continue to co-parent and show our children a healthy way to let each other go. Were there experiences in our marriage that we could have used as a reason to hate and blame each other? Absolutely! But we chose a different path. Even now, four years out from the ending, we continue to love and support each other through our personal hardships, apart but together. It is a beautiful expression of a different kind of love. Love is love, and it has the ability within us to change the world. Each of us has the choice to choose love over fear in any situation.

I am grateful to myself that I choose the highest vibration that makes me whole.

Scarce Heart

Scarce heart chakra energy holds jealousy, resentment, grudges, fear of intimacy, and defensiveness.

Abundant Heart

Abundant heart chakra energy holds compassion, self-love, gratitude, courage, forgiveness, and trust.

LIFE RECIPE AFFIRMATION: HEART

"I am *love.*
I am *Loved.*
I am *magnetic.*"

Reflect

Are there any barriers or wounds that prevent you from fully opening your heart?

Listen

Activate, open, balance, and heal your heart chakra. Use a frequency that encourages you to restore human consciousness to its full power and potential. Sunbeams, rainbows, flowers, grass, and even the buzzing of bees vibrate at 528 hertz. Nature in balance vibrates at that same frequency. It is the frequency of life itself. More than any sound previously discovered, the "love frequency" resonates at the heart of everything. It connects your heart, your spiritual essence, to the spiraling reality of heaven and earth.

Eat

An abundant heart chakra craves naturally green foods

Green cruciferous vegetables, such as broccoli, kale, brussels sprouts, and bok choy

Green peas

Green beans

Cucumbers

Green bell peppers

Zucchini

Asparagus

Green apples

Kiwi

Green grapes

Green lentils

Edamame

Matcha

Celery

Green onions

Swiss chard

Honeydew melons

Green olives

Seaweed (such as nori or wakame)

Foods that support a healthy heart

Fish high in omega-3 fatty acids, such as salmon, mackerel, sardines, trout, and tuna

Berries

Whole grains

Avocados

Almonds

Walnuts

Legumes

Olive oil

Foods that make you feel loved

Ancestral foods that make you feel close to your heritage, or something cooked by a beloved relative

Foods you loved as a child

Food prepared for you by someone who loves you, or food you prepare to share with a loved one

Green spices such as basil, cilantro, mint, and parsley

93

Made with love, of course.

Hello, Heart Smoothie

INGREDIENTS

Granny Smith apples peeled—who is "Granny Smith," anyway? Or you can call them "Glamma Vie" apples.

1 cup of baby kale, packed—decide if you want more or less kale. Perhaps spinach?

1/2 cup of fresh pineapple—remember, size doesn't matter!

1/2 cup of frozen mango—or be my guest and peel that fresh mango!

Splash of water

HOW TO ENJOY

• Combine all ingredients in a blender and blend until smooth.

Hello, Heart Spicy Avocado Toast

INGREDIENTS

1 ripe avocado—remember to wash the skin of your avocado

1 tablespoon of lemon juice

1 bagel or bread of your choice—make sure it's a healthy, fiber-filled bread with no added sugar

Salt and pepper to taste

Diced cucumber to taste

Green jalapeño to taste—add more spice if you like! The spice of life is nice!

HOW TO ENJOY

- Scoop the avocado into a bowl and use a fork to mash the avocado to your desired consistency.

- Add lemon juice and mix well.

- Toast the bread of your choice to your preferred level of crispness. Set aside.

- Prepare your favorite garnishes and set them aside.

- Once the bread is toasted, spread the avocado mixture evenly over each slice.

- Top the avocado toast with your prepared garnishes.

Love Note

*Serve immediately with a knife and fork and fun napkin
that brings you joy! And say hello to your heart!*

Wear

The energetic expression is the harmonious balance between masculine and feminine energy. By embracing the properties of the heart chakra color in your life's daily style, you will begin to embody the compassionate energy you wish to incorporate on the inside. It's an easy way to begin training your mind to receive more abundance in this area of your life.

Accessorize with the color green, heart symbols, handmade with love items, sustainably made materials, gifted items, and mindfully select brands that give back.

Decorate

Enriching your home with vibrant shades of soothing green plants—or even decor resembling green accents in nature— channel the loving spirit of the greatest nurturing mother, Mother Nature. I love to pick up stones resembling hearts and use them as gifts or everyday decor.

CHAPTER 8

SPEAK YOUR MIND, FIND YOUR TRUTH

THROAT CHAKRA

For much of my life, I remained in a state of inner quietness—not literally, but in the realm of self-expression. It wasn't until recently that I realized the profound silence that lived within me, the absence of my own voice. I didn't grasp the concept that I could hold opinions, make choices, and forge paths without external validation. I lived under the impression that my decisions needed approval—that others held the mic, and I had to listen. My desires were secondary to the voices around me.

The idea of having an opinion about my own future seemed like a distant dream. I didn't recognize my own capacity to set boundaries, to assert myself, to declare what I truly wanted. Instead, it was as if someone else held the reins to my narrative, dictating the plot and the dialogue. In that silence, I felt a scarcity—a lack of fulfillment and authenticity that left me feeling incomplete. As I journeyed through life, I began to open to the realization that self-expression isn't a luxury reserved for the privileged few; it's an inherent right, an abundant reservoir waiting to be tapped into. It's the freedom to paint the canvas of existence with the vibrant hues of our thoughts, desires, and emotions. It's the power to shape our destinies, to carve out our identities without fear or inhibition.

In embracing my voice, I discovered a richness, wealth, and abundance—a tapestry of experiences waiting to be woven, created, and manifested. In this new realization I found liberation—I had released myself from the shackles of silence and discovered the boundless possibilities that lie within me.

Abundant self-expression goes beyond just speaking up—it's about every facet of who we are. It's in the way we dress, the vibe we create in our homes, and even the company we keep. For the longest time, I was lost in this sea of conformity. I didn't really know myself, so I figured I had to blend in, follow the crowd. My business, my style, even my thoughts—I thought they had to mirror everyone else's.

But then, as I started to find my footing, I realized that I didn't have to fit into anyone else's mold. I could dress how I wanted, decorate my space with things that spoke to me, and surround myself with people who truly understood me. It's like I finally gave myself permission to be authentic, to have my own opinions, my own way of doing things. And let me tell you, that sense of freedom is like a breath of fresh air after being stifled for so long. It's about embracing the uniqueness that makes me, well, me.

It Wasn't Me

It was just another ordinary morning in my world. The sun lazily crept through the curtains, signaling the start of another monotonous day. The alarm clock blared, and I begrudgingly dragged myself out of bed, knowing that the daily grind awaited me. School.

My sister, Charlotte had the unfortunate task of catching an ungodly early bus at 6:50 a.m., while I, being the lucky one, could enjoy a few more precious minutes of sleep before facing the day. I want to add that she returned home from her school later than me.

Charlotte was always the cool one in our family, effortlessly stylish in her choice of clothes. Preppy was the genre of choice, and I wanted to be preppy just like her. I couldn't help but envy her fashion sense, but borrowing her outfits without permission always ended in disaster.

So one day, I decided to take matters into my own hands. Charlotte had gone to our dad and requested a padlock for her door, a fortress to protect her coveted wardrobe. But I wasn't one to be deterred. I concocted a plan to crack the code and unlock the fashion treasures hidden behind that padlocked door.

With determination and a touch of mischief, I armed myself with a trusty screwdriver and set out to conquer the fashion world. I knew I had a small window of opportunity while Charlotte was away, and I was determined to seize it. Little did she know, her clothes were about to embark on a wild adventure, courtesy of her sneaky little sister.

With precision, I was able to unlock the padlock. It was like I was walking straight into heaven. All my dream clothes were right in front of me, and I felt like I had just won the lottery. How would I choose? Where would I begin? I had argyle sweaters in a multitude of colors. I had pants printed with pink and green patterns—remember we were sporting preppy looks back then. I could even choose my favorite color espadrilles to match the ensemble. I made my final decision—a pink sweater with pink lily pad and green frog cotton pants and neutral espadrilles. At last, I was feeling pretty darn fine!

As I strolled into school, adorned in my new outfit, I felt so confident. Each step I took seemed lighter; my posture was taller, as if I had transformed into a version of Charlotte herself. Throughout the day, I navigated my classes with a newfound swagger, my head held high, and a subtle skip in my step, betraying my inner joy.

As the final bell chimed, I made my way to the bus stop, still basking in the glow of my self-assurance. Thoughts of slipping back into my usual attire flitted through my mind, but I relished the idea of prolonging this feeling for just a little while longer.

However, fate had other plans in store for me. Just as I approached the front door of my home, ready to execute my discreet wardrobe change, I was greeted by an unexpected sight—my sister, home from school earlier than usual. Caught off guard, I froze in my tracks, the weight of guilt settling in my stomach as I realized my secret was about to be exposed.

With a sinking heart, I entered the house, trying in vain to conjure up a plausible excuse for the deviation from my normal attire. But as I stood before my sister, her expression was a mix of anger and betrayal. I knew that my attempt to conceal my little fashion experiment had been futile. There was no denying it—I had been caught red-handed.

Fast Forward to Today

I do not borrow my sister's clothes, nor do I resonate with the preppy style. My journey toward embracing my true essence has been marked by a significant shift in the way I express myself through clothing.

There was a time when I sought validation from external sources, relying on body-hugging attire to feel a fleeting sense of confidence. My wardrobe choices were dictated by the need to conform to societal standards and garner approval from others. But as I embarked on a path of self-discovery, I gradually shed the shackles of external validation.

Nowadays, my fashion choices are solely a reflection of my inner self, guided by a newfound

sense of liberation. With each garment I select, I am no longer seeking validation or approval from anyone else but myself. It's a liberating feeling, to dress for the sheer joy of it, without the burden of others' opinions weighing me down.

Embracing my authentic self has allowed me to cultivate a cool, relaxed vibe that resonates with the abundant frequency I exude. Gone are the days of conforming to societal norms—I now revel in the freedom to express myself authentically through my clothing, radiating confidence from within.

Expression Is Laughter

Laughter was a missing piece in the puzzle of my self-expression. My mother was English and would always say to me, "I can't stand the giggling, Sarah!" Even that, the simple act of laughter, was something I couldn't fully embrace. It's funny, really, because laughter is supposed to be this natural, spontaneous thing, right? But for me, it was like there was an invisible force holding me back, stifling even the most genuine moments of joy.

I remember my best friend, Grace. Whenever she came over for a sleepover, it was as if we had this unspoken agreement to suppress our laughter. We'd sit at the dining room table with my family, trying our best to maintain composure, but the moment our eyes met, it was game over. We'd dissolve into fits of giggles, unable to contain ourselves.

The thing is, it wasn't just the fear of getting in trouble with my mom that held me back, although that was definitely part of it. It was also this sense of . . . I don't know, guilt maybe? I believed I wasn't supposed to be enjoying myself too much, or that being silly was somehow wrong. But in those moments with Grace, I realized how freeing it was to just let go—to laugh until our sides hurt without worrying about judgment or consequence.

Looking back, I see that those moments of shared laughter were some of the most precious times of my life. They were a reminder that joy isn't something to be contained or suppressed—it's something to be celebrated, embraced, and shared with those we hold dear.

The more abundant energy I felt, the more I started to unravel the layers of inhibition. I began to realize just how essential laughter is. It's not just about amusement; it's about connection, release, and pure, unadulterated happiness. So, bit by bit, I allowed myself to let go—to chuckle at the absurdities of life, to giggle at the silliness of my own mistakes, and to share in the infectious joy of those around me.

And you know what? It's as if I finally found my voice in laughter—a voice that doesn't need words to express itself, a voice that speaks volumes in its simplicity. It has become a cornerstone of my self-expression, a reminder that life is meant to be lived with a light heart and a hearty laugh. I see my life now through a sparkly lens, through childlike eyes even at my beautiful age of sixty. The most beautiful expression of myself is sharing this with others.

Self-Expression Can Transcend the World

Last October, I embarked on a journey to Egypt, leading a group of nine other women on what would become a truly transformative travel experience for us all. Among our many adventures was a visit to Faiyum, a remote area nestled amidst the enchanting Magic Lake and the vast expanse of the Sahara Desert. It was here that we encountered the Bedouins traveling the rugged terrain with entire families on motorcycles, a sight that spoke volumes about the resilience of the human spirit.

On that crisp morning, as the sun began its rise in the sky, we set out for the desert in three cars to experience dune jumping. We were accompanied by our drivers and an armed security guard whom I later learned was named Ahmed. Despite our shared journey to the dunes, Ahmed remained somewhat of a mystery to me. He spoke no English and maintained a stoic demeanor, clad in his black suit, collared shirt, and that imposing semi-automatic gun strapped to his belt.

As we ventured deeper into the heart of the desert dunes, I couldn't shake the feeling that perhaps a touch of whimsy was needed amidst the seriousness of our surroundings and the world's current events. The Israel–Hamas war had just broken out, and the mood of the world was dark. So, before we embarked on our adventure, I reached into my bag and pulled out ten pairs of glasses adorned with glittering frames. I just happened to throw them in my bag before we left that morning—a small, spontaneous gesture to inject some joy into our expedition.

I distributed the glasses to everyone present, including our drivers and, of course, Ahmed. The transformation that ensued was nothing short of magical. The once-buttoned-up security guard's demeanor softened as he slipped on a pair of pink glasses, the glitter twinkling around his eyes. Suddenly, the weight of his responsibilities seemed to lift, replaced by an infectious sense of childlike wonder.

With a wide grin on his face, Ahmed began to giggle uncontrollably, his laughter echoing against the vast desert landscape. He even joined in a spirited Arabic song, his leg dangling out of the car window as he clapped along to the rhythm. In that moment, it was as though the barriers of language and culture dissolved, and we were simply a group of kindred spirits basking in the joy of the present moment.

And therein lies the beauty of abundant, joyful living—the ability to radiate positive energy that transcends barriers and touches the hearts of others. In embracing our own light, we inadvertently illuminate the paths of those around us, guiding them toward their own sources of joy and authenticity.

Scarce Throat

Scarce throat chakra energy holds fear of speaking, an inability to express thoughts, social anxiety, detachment, and stubbornness.

Abundant Throat

Abundant throat chakra energy holds expression, confidence when speaking, words aligned with your truth, and great communication skills.

LIFE RECIPE AFFIRMATION: THROAT

"I am *authentic*. I am *bold*. I am *expressive*."

Reflect

How comfortable are you with speaking your truth and expressing your thoughts and feelings?

Listen

If your throat chakra is not balanced, you will be unable to express yourself and will often be misinterpreted or misunderstood by others. You will probably be "wishy washy" or considered unreliable by the people in your life. Telling the truth and being honest with yourself is something you probably have a difficult time with, and giving mixed messages is likely something that has gotten you into trouble before. Until you find balance within the throat chakra, your life will remain the same—and nothing will ever work out in the way you would like it to.

Eat

Naturally blue foods
Blueberries
Blackberries
Elderberries
Blue potatoes
Blue corn
Blue butterfly pea flower
Blue peas
Blue hubbard squash
Mussels, bluefish, and blue whiting

Foods that are soothing to the throat
Seaweed and sea vegetables
Honey
Ginger
Chamomile tea
Warm broth
Coconut water
Aloe vera juice
Marshmallow root, slippery elm, and licorice root
Mineral water or concentrated drops
Pre & probiotic mouthwash
Iodine-rich foods, Brazil nuts, seaweed, kelp

Foods that tell a story
Colorfully designed grazing boards
Edible art like decorative baked goods
Try fusing different styles or techniques
Soups, stews, and slow-cooked meals

Throat Chakra Blueberry Parfait

INGREDIENTS

1 cup of fresh or frozen blueberries, blackberries, or a combination of the two—fresh are glorious

1 tablespoon of maple syrup—go to Maine for the syrup or just get fresh and pure syrup

1 teaspoon of arrowroot powder—mix with 1 tablespoon of water to thicken

1 container of coconut yogurt, no added sugar—amount depends on how much you want to make

Wholesome granola, nuts, seeds, mint leaves, citrus zest, or even edible flowers

HOW TO ENJOY

- Place the berries and the syrup in a small saucepan and heat until the texture resembles a loose jam.

- Mix the arrowroot and water mixture into the berries and stir until the berries thicken slightly.

- Allow the mixture to cool and serve atop the coconut yogurt of your choice and garnish liberally.

Love Note

Get creative here! I love enjoying these parfaits in wooden bowls and connecting to the expression of nature.

Throat Chakra Blue Potato Soup

INGREDIENTS

3 tablespoons of coconut oil

1 onion (red or white), coarsely chopped—remember your goggles!

1 1/2 pounds of blue potatoes, peeled and quartered—yes, there are blue potatoes.

6 cups of organic vegetable stock

1 bay leaf—remember to take it out when serving! That is hard to swallow!

1 cup of coconut milk or loose coconut yogurt

1/2 teaspoon of nutmeg—a whole nutmeg grated is wonderful!

1/2 teaspoon of pepper

Pink salt to taste

Additional herbs for garnish such as dill, thyme, or rosemary

HOW TO ENJOY

* Melt the coconut oil in a large saucepan over medium heat. Sauté the onion until translucent.

* Add the potatoes, stock, and bay leaf. Bring to a boil, then cover and simmer until potatoes are fork tender. Remove the bay leaf or you may get it stuck in your throat.

* Blend with an immersion blender until smooth, taking care not to overblend or the mixture could become gluey.

* Stir in coconut milk or yogurt. Season with nutmeg, pepper, salt, and herbs of your choice.

Wear

The energetic expression is unapologetic and bold. By embracing the properties of the throat chakra color in your life's daily style, you will begin to express the energy you wish to embody on the inside. It's an easy way to begin training your mind to receive more abundance in this area of your life.

Accessorize with the color blue, fluffy (vegan) furs, daring neck glam, bright scarves, collared shirts, and don't be afraid to get funky with your choices!

Decorate

Who said a table setting or your wall decor needs to be stuffy? Express your inner self through your imaginative styling. When someone says, "It's too much," add a little more.

CHAPTER 9

FEAR IS IN THE EYE OF THE BEHOLDER

THIRD EYE CHAKRA

To me, the third eye chakra isn't just a concept; it's a sacred sanctuary in which intuition and insight intersect. It's our inner compass, guiding us toward higher understanding and broader perspectives. But embracing this idea can be daunting when fear takes the reins. Fear, with its suffocating grip, dampens our intuitive powers, casting shadows over our ability to hear the whispers of our inner wisdom.

How I See It

For much of my journey, fear was a constant companion, lurking in the corners of my mind like an unwanted guest. It held me captive, breeding worries about failure, judgment, and even scarcity. Its presence clouded my vision, making it difficult to listen to the gentle nudges from within. Yet, deep down, I knew that the third eye chakra wasn't a realm of darkness; it was a beacon of light illuminating my path, waiting for me to embrace its wisdom.

They say, "Fear is in the eye of the beholder." It's a powerful force that distorts our perception and stifles our potential. While fear is scarce, intuition is abundant. I realized that fear was the barrier blocking me from truly connecting with my inner guidance. It whispered doubts and uncertainties, urging me to dismiss the intuitive nudges guiding me toward my highest self.

My journey toward self-discovery led me to confront these fears head on. Through meditation and introspection, I peeled back the layers of fear that had woven themselves into my being. I unearthed the stories I had long identified with, realizing that these fears weren't truly mine—they were illusions obscuring my truth. Meditation saved my life.

Ironically, while I encouraged bravery in my children, I shied away from risks and opportunities that resonated with my heart's deepest desires. But as I reclaimed control over my narrative, I silenced the voices of doubt and apprehension. No longer would fear dictate the trajectory of my life; I embraced the uncertainty, trusting in the wisdom of my innermost instincts.

In releasing fear's grip, I discovered a newfound freedom—a freedom that empowered me to embark on adventures with an open heart and unwavering determination. And as I witnessed the transformative power of courage and self-belief, I found solace in knowing that fear could be conquered by the radiance of self-discovery and self-assurance.

Meditation Saved My Life: The Turning Point and Changing the Relationship with Fear

One huge turning point in my life, when I truly began to hear the whispers of my own intuition, came when I made that difficult decision to end my thirty-year marriage. It wasn't an easy choice, and for the last decade of those thirty years, I found myself continuously pushing aside my own needs and desires, letting fear hold the power over my actions. I would say to myself, "It's going to get better. Just hang in there and be quiet." I remember those years vividly—the quiet but persistent nudges from within, urging me to listen, to acknowledge my own truth. Yet, time and again, I chose to ignore them, allowing fear to maintain its tight grip on the steering wheel of my life. It was as though I was stuck in a loop, trapped in a cycle of hesitation and self-doubt.

But as the years passed, those whispers grew louder, more insistent, until they could no longer be ignored. It was as if my inner voice was pleading with me to break free from the constraints that bound me, to embrace the uncertainty of the unknown with courage and conviction. The children were all out of the house and making their own way, so there were no more excuses. It was time. And so, with a mixture of trepidation and determination, I made the courageous decision to walk away from a marriage that no longer aligned with my deepest truths and highest vision.

Leaving behind the comfort and familiarity of three decades of companionship was undoubtedly one of the most challenging decisions I've ever made. Yet, in doing so, I embarked on a journey of profound

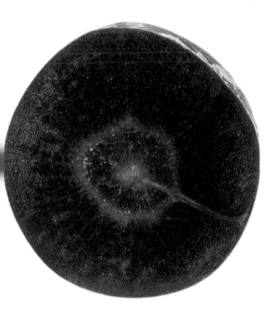
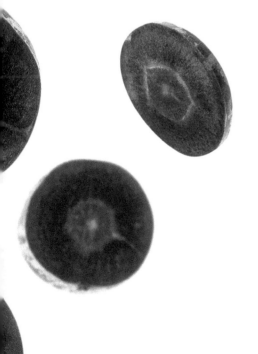

self-discovery and empowerment—a journey guided by the unwavering belief that I deserved happiness and fulfillment.

Choosing to listen to my intuition and follow its guidance was a transformative act of self-love and liberation. It was a declaration of independence from the fears and insecurities that had held me back for so long. And though the path ahead was uncertain, I stepped forward with newfound courage and determination, trusting in the wisdom of my innermost self.

In embracing the unknown, I discovered a newfound sense of freedom and authenticity—a freedom to live life on my own terms, guided by the whispers of my intuition. And as I navigated the twists and turns of this new chapter, I found solace in the knowledge that, by honoring my own truth, I was paving the way for a brighter, more fulfilling future.

Fear Sometimes Reappears

Even when we believe we've mastered our understanding of fear, there are moments when it rears its head in unexpected ways, delving into deeper layers of our psyche. I experienced this firsthand. Leading up to my trip to Egypt, an old acquaintance called Fear resurfaced from the depths of my past with each step closer to departure. This time, its presence was particularly potent, evoking a sense of déjà vu that was both unsettling and familiar. Yet, amidst the rising tide of apprehension, I discovered a newfound resilience. It was a resilience born from a practice I've come to rely on—something I call "fear setting." Fear setting isn't about banishing fear altogether; it's about understanding its grip and learning to navigate through it. As I stood on the edge of a thirteen-hour journey to a foreign land, I found solace in this practice. It wasn't about denying the fear or pretending it didn't exist. Instead, it was about acknowledging its presence and making a conscious choice to move forward despite it.

With each step toward the departure gate, I confronted my fears head on, dissecting them into manageable pieces. First, I had to get quiet and ask myself what I was afraid of, specifically. I identified the worst-case scenarios, recognizing that they were often far less formidable than they initially seemed. What came to me were these fears: I would be embarking to a place I had never visited before—fear of the unknown. I was afraid of being away from my partner for almost three weeks—fear of abandonment. I was afraid of listening to my own intuition, even though many people were telling me not to go as the Israel-Hamas war had just broken out—fear of being judged by others. By breaking down the barriers of fear, I liberated myself to embrace the adventure that was before me. Fear was no longer in charge. At that moment I became bigger than my fear.

And so, armed with a newfound sense of empowerment, I boarded that plane bound for Egypt. The journey wasn't just a physical one—it was a testament to the power of resilience and the triumph of the human spirit over fear.

Fear Setting Practice to Abundance, in Detail

1. Draw three columns on a sheet of paper. The first column is the Define column. The second column is the Prevent column. The final column is the Repair column.

2. Write down the fear stories you are telling yourself. Rate them on a scale of 1 to 10. List out your most scary scenarios, your doubts, and your what ifs. Write it all down, and don't hold back. What's the worst-case scenario? What might go wrong? Go deep here.

3. The Repair column is where you will begin to see the abundant light. How could you make those stories better? What actions could you take?

4. On the back of this paper, write down what listening to the fear would cost you. What would you miss out on if you didn't do what was scaring you?

When we let our stories flow from our sixth chakra, we unleash a powerful force within us, lifting us to new heights and allowing our inner wisdom to guide us. It's like tuning into our own vibe, our own authentic frequency that we are all born with. Our intuition reaches its peak, paving the way for us to manifest the dreams we long for. Embracing and understanding our inner stories isn't just about letting go; it's about stepping into our own power, shaping a life that's truly ours, filled with purpose and endless opportunities.

Scarce Eye

Scarce third eye chakra energy holds headaches, sleep issues, a lack of focus, a lack of spiritual awareness, and negative thinking.

Abundant Eye

Abundant third eye chakra energy holds a higher state of consciousness, connection to your truth, connection to spirit, and trust in self.

LIFE RECIPE AFFIRMATION: THIRD EYE

"I am a *visionary*. I am *intuitive*. I am *clear*."

Reflect

Are there moments when you ignored your intuition and later wished you had listened?

Listen

The chakra of our intuition is the brow chakra. Unblocking this chakra opens the massive power and hidden potential we all have within us. This chakra is our guiding light, our doorway to the subtle messages we receive from the universe. Unblocking this chakra allows us to trust our inner guiding light more than anything else in this world. Rather than looking outward, this chakra guides us inward to look for the answers we are searching outward.

Eat

To nourish your third eye chakra, try naturally purple foods

- Purple grapes
- Purple cabbage
- Purple carrots
- Purple cauliflower
- Purple sweet potatoes
- Eggplant
- Açaí berries
- Black rice
- Plums
- Purple figs
- Purple kale

Foods that support healthy eye function

- Leafy green vegetables
- Carrots of any color
- Citrus fruits
- Fish and other lean proteins
- Nuts and seeds
- Eggs
- Bell peppers
- Legumes

Foods that support intuition

- Berries
- Dark chocolate
- Turmeric
- Avocados
- Green tea
- Fermented foods
- Herbs such as mugwort, lavender, chamomile, valerian, peppermint, sage, and rosemary

Intuitive Sutra Smoothie

INGREDIENTS

1 1/2 fresh or frozen bananas

1 cup of fresh or frozen blueberries

1/2 cup of fresh or frozen blackberries

1 1/2 teaspoons of spirulina—available in any health food store near you. It's full of nutrients that are so healing.

1 cup of fresh or frozen pineapple, cut up

1 cup of water

HOW TO ENJOY

- Combine all ingredients into a blender and blend until smooth.

Third Eye Energy Bars

INGREDIENTS

7 large Medjool dates, pitted—it's important that they have no pits! Or you'll have no teeth.

1/2 cup of blueberries—you can also use dried blueberries

2 tablespoons of poppy seeds, dried

2 tablespoons of raisins, not golden— you can omit if you're cutting your sugar intake

1 tablespoon of raw pumpkin seeds

1 tablespoon of hemp seeds

1/4 teaspoon of cinnamon

Optional—A sprinkling of chopped oats

HOW TO ENJOY

- Process all ingredients in a food processor into a chunky mixture.
- Line a 6-by-6 glass dish, pressing the mixture down evenly into the dish.
- Notice how beautiful it is before you cut it into nine even squares and enjoy it.

Love Note

A perfect snack, especially for kids who aren't finicky.

*W*ear

The energetic expression is courageous, self-assured, and intuitive. By embracing the adventurous properties of the third-eye chakra color in your life's daily style, you will begin to develop the energy you wish to embody on the inside. It's an easy way to begin training your mind to receive more abundance in this area of your life.

Accessorize with the color indigo, use symbols of the third eye, head-turning glasses and sunglasses, circular symbols, and incorporate eye-catching sheer, lace, or chiffon materials.

Decorate

Use decor like a snow globe or a crystal ball to symbolize the gift of sight and the clarity of mind. Drink water or fancy mocktails from beautiful crystal-clear glasses, or use garnishes or shaped ice in a unique way.

CHAPTER 10

CROWNING GLORY

CROWN CHAKRA

The depth of spirituality and finding that sweet spot in the crown chakra signal the peak of our energy journey. When our crown chakra is in tune, it's like plugging into something greater than ourselves, connecting with the universe in a profound way. It opens doors to deeper understanding, clarity, and a sense of purpose that goes beyond the everyday grind. This balance allows us to rise above petty stuff, bringing a sense of inner peace, satisfaction, and a feeling of being in sync with something much bigger than ourselves. When our energy centers align, that's when we truly connect with ourselves—the essence of who we were meant to be. The crown chakra serves as the sacred roof of our energy connectivity, crowning our spiritual home in completeness.

My Spiritual Abundance Found

My life has been a path of discovery. I am a white woman who was raised in a typical American family with a yard and a white-picket fence—we actually had the fence. Church or religion was never a part of my younger impressionable years. As children, my siblings and I were not shown whom or what to believe in. I saw my friends and their families practicing their organized religion. What was wrong with me? Why didn't I have this unity? I would witness them dressed in their Sunday best and driving to their nearest congregation in their beloved neighborhood church. I struggled to not feel left out. My best friend throughout elementary school and high school was from a strict Catholic family. I would sit at the dinner table with her seven brothers in their small suburban home and felt somehow left out and awkward when her father would lead the dinner prayer and the Trinitarian formula. I was worried that if I did it wrong, I would end up being cursed for the rest of my life for not crossing my chest in the proper direction. My father used to make fun of that formula and say, "Father, Son, and the Holy Cow." I didn't know that this practice was one of the central Christian affirmations about

God. I had no connection to any god back then. I just wanted to fit in with my friends and feel included.

The only thing I knew growing up was that my father had an aversion to anything associated with a higher power or an understanding of faith. I still don't know the exact details of what my father experienced, but he had a traumatic event with the church that forever altered his life. There were some intimate stories revealed when my father and his then-third wife were having difficulties in their marriage. He experienced this trauma while he was an altar boy. He was not one to run to the nearest therapy office to talk about anything that happened to him, so the trauma and pain was stuffed down into that false place of security. The rumors of sexual abuse with priests and altar boys were similar to what plagues the news today. I have to switch off the news when I hear any of these atrocities. It's as if I was the one to have experienced it. I have to remind myself that I am carrying the pain of his past in my DNA. His unhealed trauma was mine. I have always wanted to understand what was behind his hatred toward any type of organized religion.

I can picture him now as a young, skinny youth, involuntarily spreading frankincense smoke as he walked down the aisle of his mothers' beloved church. St. Michael's Episcopal Church had a tall wooden steeple and golden weathervane. It stood at the top of the town, overlooking the unassuming homes dating back to 1619 and the harbor. The large red wooden doors welcomed anyone wanting the comfort of worship. The backs of the pews were upright. For the parishioners, there never was a comfortable way to sit. I can picture my father walking down the aisle. His frail innocence cloaked in the traditional white robe that altar boys wore, not knowing where to rest his eyes in the congregation in fear of yet another adult's frowning disapproval. I can feel his sadness thinking he wasn't able to find his own spiritual path. As an adult now, I experienced the freedom to choose what felt right for me. I am grateful he gave me this choice, even though it came from the trauma of his past. He gave me that choice by avoiding any feelings from his past. There was no time for that. His dominant mother was a prominent figure in his small town of Marblehead, Massachusetts. He had to do the right thing—smile when prompted; dress in an appropriate white button-down shirt, bow tie, and black slacks; slick his hair perfectly to one side. The clothes were to uphold the family's impeccable image. His two younger brothers watched his every move. My father's youth was plagued with expectations. He was told what to do. He was told what to believe. This was his inner scarcity growing within him.

There was no place to hide in this tight-knit town where brightly colored clapboard homes overlooked a small harbor of sail boats awaiting their owners to hoist their sails. Buried underneath this seemingly angelic town will be a truth I will never know—the truth of his religion that shaped me and my siblings into our adulthood. I witnessed this unresolved pattern of his youth in our family. The dominance in his mother was the safety that he sought in his three marriages when making decisions, expressing his opinion, or earning

money. If I would have known the pain in my father's early life, perhaps my behavior toward him would have been different growing up. I didn't understand his angry outbursts in our kitchen after we finished our eating together. My bedroom was a wall away from the noise of the pots and pans being thrown into the sink. The noisy banging and his shouting voice collided with each other. I had to cover my ears at night with my pillow, so as not to hear his angry episodes. He must have felt great loneliness sleeping alone in his attic room away from my mother. One night there was a terrible fight in which my parents never shared a bed again. I never knew what the cause of this horrific night was. I can remember trying to stuff notes under my parents' door while the shouting escalated. I wanted to let them know that I loved them. What I needed at that moment was security and an abundance of emotional love. Both of my parents were feeling the trauma and pain that they experienced in their own lives. I instead found safety from my stuffed animals that sat slumped on the end of my bed—a constant anchor of security and a connection to something outside of myself. I had my stuffed rabbit with the blue smock and floppy ears; Froggy, whose insides were seeping out of his torso; and my orange fox that I bought in a gift shop in England.

It is only now that I understand the pain he must have been feeling throughout his life. I can remember trying to sit with him and gently touching his hand when my family and I would visit him and his then-wife in Maine. Their house was a peaceful sanctuary nestled along a private beach in Harpswell. When he was confronted with my kindness, he would quickly make an excuse and busy himself with a task on his endless to-do list. He was not able to feel comforted and loved even by his daughter.

His rejective path to religion led each of his three children to be raised without any specific sect to follow. This reluctance led me to feelings of insecurity whenever I was in the presence of families that were cemented in their beliefs. I felt like an outcast and was left feeling spiritually and emotionally scarce.

My beliefs were that of a free spirit.

As I entered adulthood, I searched for a higher power with which I could feel a sense of connection. I longed to feel a sense of security and wholeness, but I was unwilling to follow the belief of someone else.

God and Jesus just didn't feel in alignment with my spirit. I never liked the way religion was a specific set of organized beliefs and practices shared by a community or group.

I didn't know it then, but what I was feeling in alignment with was spirituality; the individual practice that has more to do with having a sense of peace and purpose, having my higher power be a beacon of light toward myself. I was on the journey at the tender age of ten. I can remember kneeling when I was afraid and talking to a spirit when I felt alone. Who was I talking to? What answers was I searching for? Was it comfort and belonging to something higher than myself?

The last attempt to find what I was looking for in a Christian church was in my small town on the eastern shore of Maryland. After the passing of my mother in 2001, I searched for a place of peace and direction. With my four children under the age of six, driving down the winding roads near our family home in Chesapeake City, I found a quaint Episcopal church that stood in a wooded lot and dated back to the early 1900s. Large oak trees offered the structure shade from the hot Maryland summers. Thoroughbred stud farms surrounded the small stone church in the springtime. Foals frolicked in the fields nearby while their mothers grazed patiently beside them. The church's window allowed me to peek outside to watch their playful dance when the sermon became uninteresting.

My four young children wiggled in the uncomfortable wooden pews. The organ was played by a woman with her hair in a well-kept bun that rested perfectly on the top of her head. She was dressed in a practical flowered dress with a lace collar, and her shoes were black and flat enough to manipulate the organ pedals. The deep notes coming from the metal pipes were comforting and reminded me of the old stone churches I used to attend in the English countryside while visiting my mother's village in Somerset, England. She had returned to her native country after my parents divorced. The stone walls gently cradled the deep tones coming from the chamber above our heads. The sound of the music was the only comfort I found inside these walls of worship.

After a few Sundays at this church, I was feeling a sense of comfort and connection. I decided I wanted to become a member. I spoke to the priest with a white beard who wore a white frock with the red cross embroidered on his sash. He conducted the morning sermons with precision and clarity. My youngest son was strapped into his baby carrier on the front of my chest. Instead of welcoming me and my young family into the church with open arms, I was told that a baptism record or certificate was required to be considered. It seemed that a silly piece of paper was to become my identity. I told him that I was baptized in England and had no way of finding the required paperwork as the ceremony happened almost forty-five years ago. With a perplexed expression, the priest apologized and said there was nothing else he could do. He added that he could help me find the documentation. I felt rejected. I was still healing the false story from my past that something was wrong with me. I was being rejected, even in a place that invites all and never judges. Right! What was not abundant was having the door slammed in my face. I never searched for that document. I never joined a church. This was not meant to be.

This was my final attempt to become part of any religious establishment. I knew there was something deeper for me than this. I have never been one to follow groups or be told what I could or couldn't believe in. This gatekeeping was guiding me to my inner light. Back then I felt unseen and confused, but now I know why this was all happening for me. I tell you this to show you how the seeds of spiritual scarcity were planted for me. The beginning of it all.

My First Spiritual Mentor

In my search for my spiritual truth, ten years ago female deities began to feel aligned with my own highest power. Their spiritual energy was attracting me like a moth to a flame. It felt so right. The path became clear. I began to connect deeper to my quiet center. Meditation helped me to tap into my authentic self and to a feeling that was void of resistance. The essence that I was born with. Abundance was my true nature.

I am a healer by trade and by purpose. Showing others their own light now that I have found mine. Be the energy first, then we will attract the physical form outside of ourselves. With the energy and healing I have experienced throughout my life, I can say that I am love and compassion. Quan Yin continues to remind me of just that. Her symbol in my home is my anchor. I became her. If we want to attract or manifest something specific in our lives, we must become the energy. I became the energy that she represents. That is abundance.

Who Is Lakshmi?

On this healing path and my search for my own idea of spirituality and inner abundance, my next spiritual anchor was Lakshmi. The image of the goddess Lakshmi came to mind as I sat in deep meditation. What? Wait! Why was this image of this beautiful woman coming to my mind? The more I meditated and released the old, limited stories, the more I connected to my quiet center. In that quiet center was my truth. Not the truth of someone else's pain and unhealed trauma. Her image was so clear. I was introduced to her image as I studied many spiritual books. This beautiful creature draped in a red sari, adorned with gold ornaments, seated on a lotus, surrounded by opulence and wealth, was there now to heal one of my deepest energetic scars. "How could this spiritual exchange be possible?" I thought to myself. I am a normal Western woman living in a traditional American family with a white-picket fence. This was not the norm I witnessed as a child or how I watched others worship. This deity, like Quan Yin, felt so right. I could feel the energy of my body relax and open to her. I was moved by the presence and richness of her feminine energy. Lakshmi is the goddess of wealth, fortune, power, luxury, beauty, fertility, and auspiciousness. She holds the promise of material fulfillment and contentment. Her energy grants wishes to those who desire to heal.

Lakshmi represents abundance for all of us. The images and stories of gods and goddesses are a part of Hindu homes and business establishments.

The world may have changed, but the thirst for material comfort continues to form

the core of most human aspirations. The way I define her is the essence of our eternal beingness. She represents what we are already. Returning to our core essence is what we all are desiring. I have used the visual anchor for many years now and offer the same to my clients who desire to live with this energetic, passionate, and abundant life. Anchors have helped me to remember the path I have committed to. Whenever I look at the faces of Quan Yin or Lakshmi, I remember who I am energetically. We can use anchors in any stage of our journeys.

Your spiritual grounding can take many forms beyond those I've mentioned. It might manifest as a cherished photograph that evokes a profound sense of connection whenever you glance at it. Or perhaps it is an object imbued with personal significance. The beauty of your spiritual grounding lies in its uniqueness to you; it's about crafting your own emblem of spiritual abundance. Whether it's a symbol, a memento, or a quiet moment of reflection, the essence remains the same: the realization that your spiritual wealth resides within you, waiting to be acknowledged and embraced. So, delve into the depths of your soul, and uncover the treasures that await—the richness and abundance of your spirit knows no bounds.

Scarce Crown

Scarce crown chakra energy holds an unwillingness to open to new ideas, dissociation with your body, and being disconnected and ungrounded.

Abundant Crown

Abundant crown chakra energy holds a connection to something greater than ourselves, cosmic consciousness, selflessness, compassion, and a connection to a higher purpose.

LIFE RECIPE AFFIRMATION: CROWN

"I am *guided*. I am *open*. I am *Light*."

Reflect

What steps can you take to nurture a sense of peace, purpose, and connection in your daily life?

Listen

This is the home of our connection to the cosmos, that infinite energy. Awakening crown chakra helps us connect with that one source of all of us. The source from which we all originated. When you meditate, think about the energy with which you resonate and bring that force within you.

$\mathcal{E}at$

Foods that nourish your connection to the universe

These foods are more about the how than the what—how they're produced, how you spend time cooking them, how you spend time enjoying them.

Focus on ethically produced foods: foods grown within the supportive cycles of nature, foods grown with empowering and eco-friendly farming practices, and foods that connect you more deeply to the place you live.

Consider cooking as a moving meditation. Turn off all distractions including television, music, or podcasts. Focus on the single action before you, giving your full awareness to washing, chopping, or stirring.

Practice eating as a ritual. Before your first bite, close your eyes and rest in gratitude for what is about to nourish you. Try closing your eyes again as you chew, giving your full awareness to the vibration of the beautiful food in your mouth.

Return to gratitude after eating, and seal the meal with a mantra, prayer, or affirmation. I love, "I hold gratitude for my deep connection to the universe."

Nourish an abundant crown chakra with naturally white foods

Cauliflower
Greek or coconut yogurt
White quinoa
Alliums such as garlic and onions
Oyster, button, king trumpet, and lion's mane mushrooms
Tofu
Coconuts
White beans
White roots such as parsnips and turnips
White rice and rice noodles, in moderation
Celeriac
White fish, like cod, haddock, and halibut or white shellfish

Foods that support healthy brain function

Turmeric
Broccoli
Avocados
Spinach
Beets
Olive oil
Flaxseeds
Dark berries
Walnuts and foods rich in omega-3 fatty acids
Pumpkins and pumpkin seeds
Dark green vegetables
Eggs
Nuts
Oranges
Dark chocolate

Crown Chakra Coconut Yogurt Chia Pudding

INGREDIENTS

1/2 cup of coconut yogurt, no added sugar

2 tablespoons of chia seeds

3 tablespoons of coconut milk, no sugar added

1 teaspoon of honey or maple syrup

Coconut flakes, fruit, or honey for garnish

HOW TO ENJOY

- Combine coconut yogurt, chia seeds, coconut milk, and honey or maple syrup in a small bowl. Mix carefully until there are no clumps.

- Place in the fridge for at least 1 hour.

Love Note

I like to make mine the night before and have it ready to go for breakfast the next morning!

Crown Chakra Angel Piña Colada

INGREDIENTS

3 cups of fresh or frozen pineapple,
  cut into chunks

2 cups of unsweetened coconut milk

1 tablespoon of fresh lime juice—
  smell that abundance!

1/8 teaspoon of almond or vanilla
  extract

Optional: the rum of your choice

HOW TO ENJOY

- Combine all ingredients in a blender; mix until smooth. Spike with a bit of rum for a boozy treat.

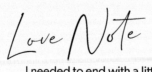

Love Note

I needed to end with a little fun!

Wear

The energetic expression of pure alignment in mind, body, and spirit. Content and connected to Divine. By embracing the adventurous properties of the third-eye chakra color in your life's daily style, you will begin to develop the energy you wish to embody on the inside. It's an easy way to begin training your mind to receive more abundance in this area of your life.

Accessorize with the colors white and deep purple. Clear crystal or white opal accents, feathered earrings, lightweight whimsical hats, symbols of crowns, and Divinity symbols like a cross, saint, lucky talisman, or prayer beads.

Decorate

Create a magnificently rich floral centerpiece of purple or white orchids to mirror your abundant faith in your divine power. Orchids (real or silk) will bring positive energy throughout your home. Gratitude for these gorgeous floral arrangements goes out to Flowers by Mayumi in Lewes, Delaware.

PART III

INTO
SACRED
ABUNDANCE

CHAPTER 11

IT ALL ADDS UP

The way we relate to food goes far beyond simple nourishment; it's a profound reflection of who we are at our core. Our relationship with food is intertwined with our emotions, our cultural background, our beliefs, and even our sense of self-worth.

Consider how we approach food in various situations. For some, it's a source of comfort, a way to soothe stress or fill an emotional void. For others, it's a means of celebration, a way to connect with loved ones and create cherished memories around the dinner table. And for many, it's a battleground, fraught with feelings of guilt, shame, and anxiety.

Our food choices can also reveal a lot about our values and priorities. Whether we opt for locally sourced, organic produce or fast food on the go, our decisions often reflect our beliefs about health, sustainability, and the environment. Similarly, the way we prepare and enjoy meals can speak volumes about our cultural heritage and traditions, serving as a link to our ancestors and a way to honor our heritage.

But perhaps most importantly, our relationship with food reflects our relationship with ourselves—how we nourish our bodies, the care and attention we give to selecting and preparing our meals, and the respect we show for the food we consume all mirror our level of self-love and self-respect.

When we approach food with mindfulness and intention, viewing it as a source of nourishment and pleasure rather than a source of guilt or shame, we not only nourish our bodies but also nurture our souls. By cultivating a healthy relationship with food, we can cultivate a deeper sense of self-awareness, self-compassion, and ultimately, self-acceptance.

So, as you sit down to your next meal, take a moment to reflect on the deeper meaning behind your food choices. What do they reveal about who you are and what you value? And how can you cultivate a more loving and respectful relationship with food that honors both your body and your spirit?

IT REALLY IS ABOUT ALLOWING

As you stand on the threshold of this final section of the book, take a moment to pause and reflect. Can you sense a subtle shift in your energy, a soft whisper of anticipation dancing in your soul? This is your moment to fully immerse yourself in the abundance that surrounds you, to drink deeply from the wellspring of life's blessings.

Perhaps you find yourself drawn to the idea of bringing out your finest china, dusting off the delicate patterns that have been waiting patiently in the cupboard. Or maybe there's a candle tucked away, its wick untouched by flame, waiting for the perfect moment to cast its warm glow upon your world. Whatever it may be, this is your invitation to embrace the richness of life with open arms.

Abundance knows no bounds; it doesn't discriminate based on wealth or status. It's about finding joy in the simple pleasures as much as the extravagant experiences. Picture yourself seated at a table adorned with a sumptuous feast, each dish a masterpiece of flavor and color. Take a moment to drink it all in with all your senses.

These moments of abundance are not reserved for a select few—they are yours to claim, yours to savor. But the key lies in allowing yourself to fully experience them. It's about opening your heart and mind to the beauty that surrounds you, letting go of any doubts or reservations that may hold you back.

So, take a deep breath and let yourself be present in this moment. Feel the abundance coursing through your veins, filling you with a sense of gratitude and wonder. And as you continue your journey, remember that abundance is not something to be chased or sought after—it is already within you, waiting to be acknowledged and embraced. So, go on, open your arms and open your heart. Let abundance flow into every aspect of your life.

THE CHECK-IN

Abundance isn't just about one isolated aspect of your life; it's the culmination of energy flowing from every corner of your being. Picture it like a rich tapestry, woven intricately from the threads of your relationships, your health, your finances, the comfort of your home, the thrill of new experiences, your spiritual connection, and your openness to growth and transformation.

Think of your life as a grand orchestra, each area playing its unique role in creating a symphony of abundance. Your relationships provide warmth and depth, like the soul-stirring melodies of a violin. Your health sets the rhythm, pulsating with vitality and vigor, urging you to dance through life with enthusiasm and uninhibited joy.

Your financial stability forms a sturdy foundation, allowing you to build upon it and reach new heights. Your home is the cozy backdrop in which you can recharge and find solace, a sanctuary amidst the chaos of the world.

Life's adventures add spice, infusing each moment with excitement and possibility, while your spiritual connection offers guidance and wisdom, like a gentle guiding hand leading you forward.

And at the core of it all is your willingness to embrace change, to continually strive for growth and improvement in every facet of your life. Like a skilled conductor, you orchestrate this symphony, bringing together all the elements in perfect harmony.

So, as you journey through life, remember that abundance isn't limited to just one area—it's a holistic expression of your being, a celebration of all that you are and all that you can be. Embrace it fully, and let its melody resonate through every aspect of your existence.

A SIMPLE WAY TO GAUGE YOUR INNER FREQUENCY

Rate each area of your life on a scale of 1–10. 1 represents "I want to shift here"; 10 represents "Hallelujah, I'm right where I want to be." Notice what is working well and all that is out of alignment. Reflect on what you want to shift and why.

Rate Your Plate

Scan the QR code below and see where you land.

Relationship to food: 1 2 3 4 5 6 7 8 9 10

Daily mindset: 1 2 3 4 5 6 7 8 9 10

Passion and purpose: 1 2 3 4 5 6 7 8 9 10

Self-empowerment: 1 2 3 4 5 6 7 8 9 10

How I love myself: 1 2 3 4 5 6 7 8 9 10

Connection to others: 1 2 3 4 5 6 7 8 9 10

Self-expression: 1 2 3 4 5 6 7 8 9 10

Inner knowing or intuition: 1 2 3 4 5 6 7 8 9 10

Spiritual guidance: 1 2 3 4 5 6 7 8 9 10

Relationship with money: 1 2 3 4 5 6 7 8 9 10

MOVING FORWARD INTO
SACRED ABUNDANCE

Now take a small climb up the abundance ladder and see how your life will unfold. Set an intention every day to live with abundant energy. Align your thoughts, actions, and emotions with the abundance you seek. Cultivate a mindset of gratitude, noticing the prosperity that already exists in your life. Surround yourself with positive influences that uplift and inspire you. As you climb higher, let go of limiting beliefs and embrace the limitless potential within you. Trust the process and watch as your life transforms, revealing new opportunities and blessings at every step.

Make the relationship with glorious food the first step on your journey to abundance. Nourishing your body with wholesome, delicious foods is fundamental to feeling vibrant and energized. Start by choosing foods that not only satisfy your taste buds but also support your overall well-being. Experiment with new recipes and ingredients that excite you and bring joy to your meals. Pay attention to how different foods make you feel and prioritize those that leave you feeling nourished and balanced.

Develop a mindful eating practice by savoring each bite, appreciating the flavors, and being fully present during meals. This connection with food can foster a deeper sense of gratitude and abundance in your daily life. Notice how nurturing your body with healthy, delightful foods positively impacts your mood, energy levels, and overall outlook.

As you enhance your relationship with food, you'll find that this practice spills over into other areas of your life, helping you make more intentional and abundant choices. Embrace this step as a foundation for cultivating a lifestyle filled with health, happiness, and, of course, sacred abundance.

GRATITUDES

It takes the right village to shine!

Thank you to myself for my commitment, determination, and trust.

Thank you to my amazing creative brand director and friend, Danielle Codere, Free Range Unicorn LLC, for always guiding me in the right direction.

Thank you, Salvatore Borriello from Reading List Editorial and Edward Bajek from Bajek Publisher Services for rescuing me and helping me create this masterpiece.

Thank you, Sara Connell of Thought Leader Academy, who has always reminded me that I can write.

Thank you Hannah Duncan, Hey Hannah Photography, for capturing my sparkle in every photograph.

Thank you to my four children, who inspire me to shine.

Thank you to my loving partner and friends who lift me up every day.

Thank you to my Divine for the light and love I feel from within.